D1460797

SAUSSURE

SIGNS, SYSTEM, AND ARBITRARINESS

ONE WEEK LOAN

UNIVERSITY LIBRARY

2 3 FEB 2007 A

OWL

MODERN EUROPEAN PHILOSOPHY

Executive editor
RAYMOND GEUSS, COLUMBIA UNIVERSITY

Editorial board
HIDÉ ISHIGURO, KEIO UNIVERSITY, JAPAN
ALAN MONTEFIORE, BALLIOL COLLEGE, OXFORD
MARY TILES, UNIVERSITY OF HAWAII

R. M. Chisholm, *Brentano and Intrinsic Value*
Maud Marie Clark, *Nietzsche on Truth and Philosophy*
Raymond Geuss, *The Idea of a Critical Theory:
Habermas and the Frankfurt School*
Gary Gutting, *Michel Foucault's Archaeology of Scientific Reason*
Karel Lambert, *Meinong and the Principle of Independence*
Frederich Neuhouser, *Fichte's Theory of Subjectivity*
Charles Taylor, *Hegel and Modern Society*
Mary Tiles, *Bachelard: Science and Objectivity*
Robert S. Tragesser, *Husserl and Realism in Logic and
Mathematics*
Peter Winch, *Simone Weil: The Just Balance*

SAUSSURE

SIGNS, SYSTEM, AND ARBITRARINESS

DAVID HOLDCROFT

Professor of Philosophy, University of Leeds

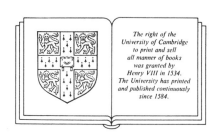

The right of the
University of Cambridge
to print and sell
all manner of books
was granted by
Henry VIII in 1534.
The University has printed
and published continuously
since 1584.

CAMBRIDGE UNIVERSITY PRESS

CAMBRIDGE

NEW YORK   PORT CHESTER   MELBOURNE   SYDNEY

NOTTINGHAM UNIVERSITY LIBRARY

Published by the Press Syndicate of the University of Cambridge
The Pitt Building, Trumpington Street, Cambridge CB2 1RP
40 West 20th Street, New York, NY 10011, USA
10 Stamford Road, Oakleigh, Melbourne 3166, Australia

© Cambridge University Press 1991

First published 1991

Printed in the United States of America

Library of Congress Cataloging-in-Publication Data
Holdcroft, David.
Saussure: signs, system, and arbitrariness / David Holdcroft.
p.   cm. (Modern European philosophy)
Includes bibliographical references (p.   ) and index.
ISBN 0-521-32618-4 (hc). ISBN 0-521-33918-9
1. Saussure, Ferdinand de, 1857–1913. 2. Linguistics. I. Title. II. Series.
P85.S18H6   1991
410'.92–dc20   90–48917
                                                                          CIP

British Library Cataloguing in Publication Data
Holdcroft, David
Saussure: signs, system, and arbitrariness.
1. Linguistic Theories of Saussure, Ferdinand de, 1857–1913
I. Title II. Series
410.92
ISBN 0 521 32618 4 hardback
ISBN 0 521 33918 9 paperback

1001170 334

Extracts and drawings from the Baskin translation of *CLG* are
reprinted with the kind permission of Peter Owen Ltd.:
Publishers.

For

EILEEN MARY

CONTENTS

PREFACE

I owe my interest in Saussure to Willie Haas, Professor of Linguistics at the University of Manchester from 1963 to 1979. Attendance at his lectures stimulated me to read the *Course in General Linguistics*, and I discussed it and structural linguistics in general with him on many enjoyable and profitable occasions. Even though I was not convinced by the structuralist methodology to which he was deeply wedded, I learnt a great deal from him; above all I remember his patience with, and forbearance of, views which attracted him not at all. Later, at the University of Warwick, I renewed that interest whilst giving a course on semiology and structuralism, which led me to appreciate Saussure's achievements not only as a linguist but also as someone whose ideas had had a major impact on the human sciences in general. The origin of the material in this book dates from lectures I gave at that time, and I owe a debt to students who attended those lectures at Warwick, Leeds, and Stony Brook for their contributions to what turned out to be an unexpectedly enjoyable course from my point of view.

I owe a debt too to colleagues at Leeds both for letting me off with a light teaching load in the autumn of 1987, which enabled me to start writing this book, and for a number of helpful discussions in seminars since then. These discussions, together with ones at the universities of Aberdeen, Edinburgh, and York helped me to clarify a number of issues. I would also like to thank the Department of Philosophy at the State University of New York at Stony Brook for providing a stimulating and relaxed atmosphere in which to work when I visited in the spring of 1988; drafts of several of the early chapters date from that time. Finally, my thanks to the editors of this series for their encouragement and help.

Leeds

INTRODUCTION

The *Course in General Linguistics* is not an easy book to read. Apart from the fact that for much of the time Saussure was preoccupied with fundamental issues about the nature of language and the methodology of linguistics, the text itself is not Saussure's but one reconstructed by Charles Bally and Albert Sechehaye from students' notes of the three lecture courses in general linguistics that he gave. The difficulties of reconstruction they faced were formidable (1.3); and though their achievement was an extraordinary one, the structure of the resulting text does not make it easy to follow Saussure's argument. This apart, he himself clearly did not think his theory as it stood was ready for publication. If at times his argument seems incomplete or inconclusive to the reader, so too it did to its author, though one can, for the most part, only guess in what respects it seemed deficient to him. Furthermore, the text has been a victim of its own success. Saussure's claim that the primary linguistic study is the study of a state of a language as it is constituted at a particular time (a so-called synchronic study) rather than one of its evolution through time (a 'diachronic' study) has come to be so widely accepted that it is hard to see how anyone could have thought otherwise. Yet much of *CLG* has to be seen as a critique of nineteenth-century historical and comparative linguistics,

1

which did indeed assume that one can engage in historical and comparative studies without grounding them in synchronic ones (1.1). This negative thrust of Saussure's argument is puzzling to a modern reader unaware of the context in which he wrote.

Accordingly, I have tried, in Chapter 1, to provide a brief description of the context in which *CLG* was written and of some of the major concerns that motivated Saussure. This account not only provides a background for the study of the text, but also outlines some of the central issues to be tackled, and tries to show what was novel and exciting about Saussure's treatment of them. Of course many of these issues recur frequently throughout this book, making it difficult to keep track of Saussure's overall position, so in Chapter 7 we return for a final assessment of these central themes in the light of the intervening discussion.

Chapter 1 concludes with a brief discussion of the text of *CLG* itself and of the very special difficulties of interpretation it poses. The editors claim that the order of the text is substantially that of the last course of lectures Saussure gave on general linguistics, the so-called Third Course; but the reality is rather more complicated, and they in fact departed from his order in a number of ways. In my view, the actual order of the Third Course is for the most part substantially clearer than the one they adopted, and the exposition of Saussure's argument in Chapters 2 to 6 of this book follows that order for this reason.

The five chapters devoted to the exposition of Saussure's argument trace the development of his central theses: first, that the primary object of linguistic study is a synchronic one, that is, one of the state of a language at a given time; and second, that a given language state is a system of arbitrary signs whose signifying properties depend entirely on their place within the system. Thus, three of the pivotal notions of that argument are those of a sign, of a system, and of arbitrariness. That is why I have used the title 'Language as a System of Signs' as the overall chapter heading for Chapters 3 to 6. Moreover – apart from the fact that if we take it as read that the signs are arbitrary, many of Saussure's major themes are neatly encapsulated – the title is one which was proposed by Saussure himself for the chapter of *CLG* in which he embarks on his theory of the sign (Part 1, Chapter 1), though it was not in fact used by the editors.

The overall argument is undoubtedly complex, and the reader may think that its exposition has not been helped by the presence of critical comments as it unfolds. Could they not have been saved to the end? Perhaps they could; but not very easily, since the point of many of the criticisms is precisely to clarify just what Saussure has to prove at a given stage to move his argument along a further step. Anyway, each chapter, except the last, concludes with a summary; and strung together, the summaries form a kind of abstract of the full discussion which will, I hope, make it easy both to relate a detailed discussion to a wider perspective and to see how it relates to the development of the overall argument. Further, to make it as easy as possible to trace the discussion of a particular theme, I have frequently cross-referenced the current one to earlier and later ones, even though the reader will no doubt discover that I do not always say the same thing in different places. Thus, the '(1.3)' in the first paragraph of this introduction refers to Chapter 1, Section 3.

SAUSSURE'S WORK
Its context and significance

That the work of Saussure, a Swiss linguist, should be the subject of a book in a series called Modern European Thought should occasion little surprise, for his subject was one to which he made a seminal contribution. What is notable is that he is an important figure not only in the development of twentieth-century linguistics, but also in that of European philosophy and the human sciences. What then distinguishes Saussure from other linguists of his generation whose work had no such impact?

Perhaps the pre-eminent difference is his concern for foundational issues, unclarity about which had been, he thought, the source of much confusion in the practice of comparative and historical linguists – the dominant nineteenth-century tradition – so much so that further progress depended on their clarification. Connected, he believed that the new conception of language that he proposed was important not simply because it cleared up confusions which had hindered the progress of linguistics itself, but also because it avoided mistakes which it was all too easy to make in the philosophy of language. So he believed that his work had important implications not only for linguistics but for philosophy too.

At first his philosophical morals had very little impact outside linguistics itself. But, as Mounin says, Saussure's work, however belatedly, affected 'and unquestionably enriched the thought of such thinkers as Merleau-Ponty, Lévi-Strauss, Henri Lefebvre, Roland Barthes, Lacan, Michel Foucault, and through them all the contemporary social sciences' (1968, 9). It is true that Mounin's claim about the impact of Saussure's work on the social sciences has to be understood to apply primarily to the continent of Europe; but its importance there for the development of structuralist thought and methodologies is unquestionable. Often the sort of enrichment of later thought that Mounin speaks of occurs without the original thinker having any prevision of the ways in which his thought might be developed in other areas by other thinkers. But this was not so in Saussure's case. He saw what he took to be the possibility of widening the scope of his methods by treating linguistics as merely a species of something more general, namely a semiological system.

For Saussure, a semiological system is any 'system of signs that express ideas' (*CLG*, 33, 16).' Natural languages are examples of such systems, but so are 'the alphabet of deaf-mutes, symbolic rites, polite formulas, military signals, etc.' Since a language is only one kind of such a system, even if it is the most important kind,

> *a science that studies the life of signs within society* is conceivable; it would be a part of social psychology and consequently of general psychology; I shall call it *semiology* (from the Greek *sēmeîon* 'sign').
> ...Linguistics is only a part of the general science of semiology; the laws discovered by semiology will be applicable to linguistics, and the latter will circumscribe a well-defined area within the mass of anthropological facts. (Ibid.)

This claim was, of course, programmatic. The laws in question were still to be discovered, so that the newly envisaged science did not then exist. But there is no doubt that in trying to define the place of linguistics in the human sciences (fig. 1.1) Saussure posited a wider space in which new enquiries might in turn find their place. However, exactly what the boundaries of this space were and what enquiries could be located there are an almost entirely conjectural matter in *CLG*; and, as we shall see later, Saussure's embryonic conception of semiology contained a number of unresolved tensions (7.4).

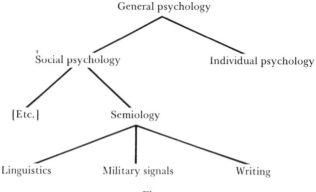

Figure 1.1

Undoubtedly, Saussure's main claim to our interest is his concern with fundamental questions about the nature of language
and the methodology of linguistics, and above all with the question of the nature of the object of linguistics itself. To understand
why these questions seemed to be of such importance to him it
is necessary to say something about the methodology of nineteenth-century linguistics, the tradition he grew up in and ultimately found wanting.

1.1. Historical concerns

In the nineteenth century, linguistics had been dominated by
comparative studies to which Saussure himself made a notable
contribution, including the work which established his reputation, *A Memoir on the Primitive Vowel Systems in Indo-European
Languages*; and it is worth remembering that he remained keenly
interested in comparative and historical questions throughout
his career. The first chapter of *CLG* is devoted to a very brief
survey of the history of linguistics, which, says Saussure, 'passed
through three stages before finding its true and unique object'
(*CLG*, 13, 1). Comparative linguistics itself corresponds to the
third of these stages; moreover, his discussion of the previous
stages is so brief by comparison that it is reasonable to infer that
he thought that the work of the comparativists was the first
empirical work done by linguists which merited serious consideration.[2]

Commenting on Bopp, the founder of this tradition, Saussure writes:

> While Bopp cannot be credited with the discovery that Sanscrit is related to certain languages of Europe and Asia, he did realize that the comparison of related languages could become the subject matter of an independent science. To illuminate one language by means of another, to explain the forms of one through the forms of the other, that is what no one had done before him. (*CLG*, 14, 2)

But although Saussure respected the aims of comparative linguists, believing that they had identified a legitimate and important field of study, he came to think that their work was methodologically confused:

> The first mistake of the comparative philologists was also the source of all their other mistakes. In their investigations (which embraced only the Indo-European languages), they never asked themselves the meaning of their comparisons or the significance of the relations that they discovered. (*CLG*, 16, 3)

Clarity demanded, Saussure came to think, that a linguist be clear whether he is dealing with different forms of the same linguistic item, e.g., the same word pronounced differently, or with different items, however closely they might resemble each other, e.g., a pair of homonyms (2.1.1). Comparisons made, often over considerable periods of time, which neglected to address these fundamental questions could well go completely astray. This in fact happened, Saussure believed, in the work of Schleicher, a comparativist who had an organicist conception of language and hence believed that languages belonging to the same kind – e.g., Greek and Sanscrit – all have to go through the same developmental stages, in the same way as plants belonging to the same species do: '...languages are natural organisms, which without being determinable by the will of man, grew and developed in accordance with fixed laws' (Schleicher 1869, 21). Such a view was, Saussure thought, incredible. As a result of it, 'language was considered a specific sphere, a fourth natural kingdom; this led to methods of reasoning that would have caused astonishment in other sciences' (*CLG*, 17, 4).

As we shall see, Saussure developed, in opposition to this view of a language as a natural object evolving in accordance with fixed laws, a conception of language as a social product, successive stages of which come about without individual or collective design (4.2, 7.3). In *CLG* he repeatedly emphasizes the social nature of languages, which he describes as a 'social fact' (*CLG*, 21, 6) which is 'outside the individual who can never create nor modify it by himself; it exists only by virtue of a sort of contract signed by the members of a community' (*CLG*, 31, 14). Elsewhere he says, 'Contrary to all appearances, language never exists apart from the social fact' and 'its social nature is one of its inner characteristics' (*CLG*, 112, 77).

Mounin has argued that this sociological dimension of Saussure's thought is one which has to be defined in relation to Durkheim. But, as we shall see (7.3), the relation of Saussure's ideas to Durkheim's is by no means straightforward, and the issue of the balance between individual and holistic elements in Saussure's thought is a delicate one.

A further inadequacy of the comparativist's approach emerges when one reflects on the fact that it was restricted to only one kind of explanation, a comparative and historical one. But how could this be ultimately satisfying? To explain the significance of a word in terms of its derivation from a word in a different language, or from a word in an earlier stage of the same language, merely raises the question of how the significance of the form from which they are derived is to be explained. If all we are restricted to is a historical explanation, then an infinite regress seems to be unavoidable.

Thus, because it failed to ask fundamental questions about its object of study, and in particular failed to ask what was being compared with what, comparative linguistics was at bottom methodologically confused. In addition, the ontological commitments of the organicist conception were in Saussure's view incredible. This conception degenerated into the speculations of Schleicher, which treat natural languages as though they are members of a species of natural object.

In the fourth stage of the history of linguistics, with which Saussure seems to have identified himself at least in part, some of the grosser confusions of the comparativists had, he thought, been cleared up. The American linguist William Dwight Whitney, who had compared a language to a social institution resting on convention, had, Saussure thought, made an important contribution. So too had the Neo-Grammarians, a school of German scholars with positivist inclinations, whose contribution had been in placing 'the results of comparative studies in their historical perspective, and thus linking the facts in their natural order' (*CLG*, 19, 5). In other words, they had not simply contented themselves with comparing different states of languages, however remote from each other they were, but had also tried to describe linguistic changes in detail and to propose mechanisms to account for them. Moreover, they had rejected the organicist conception of a language, so that 'thanks to them language is no longer looked upon as an organism that develops independently but as a product of the collective mind of linguistic groups' (ibid.).

As we saw, Saussure himself was a keen protagonist of the view that language is social; so presumably what he meant when he said that it was in this fourth and final stage that linguistics had found its true object was that it was no longer regarded, as Schleicher had regarded it, as a species of natural object, but as a social product. But lest the reader should think that there was no more fundamental work to be done, he adds that 'the neo-grammarians did not illuminate the whole question, and the fundamental problems of general linguistics still await solution' (ibid.). In other words, the clouds obliterating the landscape had lifted, but its detailed features still remained obscure, awaiting the illumination to be provided by the subsequent chapters of *CLG*, which make a decisive break with the then prevailing view that historical linguistics is the fundamental study.

1.2. Saussure and the philosophers

At first sight, the idea that Saussure addressed himself to philosophical issues is somewhat strained; a glance at the index of *CLG* shows that it does not even include 'philosophy' as a heading. Nevertheless it is possible to see a number of points at which Saussure was keenly aware of the philosophical relevance of his work. Saussure's brief history of linguistics begins by telling us that at the first of the four stages that he distinguishes 'something called "grammar" was studied. This study, initiated by the Greeks and continued mainly by the French, was based on logic' (*CLG*, 13, 1). The study in question was regarded by contemporaries as primarily philosophical. This was something he had no need to point out, since his audience would of course have understood the reference to French work of this sort as one to the tradition of general grammar, which began with the publication of Lancelot and Arnaud's *Grammaire générale et raisonnée* in 1660, often known simply as the *Port Royal Grammar*, and continued until the end of the eighteenth century.[3] So Saussure's brusque dismissal of this tradition is an index of the extent to which he distanced himself from it. Its faults were in his view many: 'It lacked a scientific approach and was detached from language itself. Its only aim was to give rules for distinguishing between correct and incorrect forms; it was a normative discipline, and its scope was limited' (*CLG*, 13, 1).

It is true that later this resolute criticism is tempered by the acknowledgment that the tradition adopted an irreproachable viewpoint from which to study language: 'Their program was strictly synchronic. The *Port Royal Grammar*, for example, attempts to describe the state of French under Louis XIV and to determine its values.... The method was then correct, but this does not mean that its application was perfect' (*CLG*, 118, 82).

However, though he thought that the viewpoint of traditional grammar was irreproachable, since its aim was to describe the state of a language at a fixed time rather than the way in which it had changed through time, his objections to its methodology and assumptions were deeply rooted. As well as the objections cited above – its normativeness, its limited scope – there was, Saussure thought, a fundamental one. This was that the traditional grammar tried to derive the structure of sentences from the logical form of thoughts, so that, for instance, to the logical categories of substance and quality there correspond the grammatical categories of noun and adjective (Ducrot 1968, 19). But such a view, Saussure came to believe, failed to recognise the autonomy of language. The structure of a language is, he argued, autonomous in the sense that it is internal to itself and not a reflection or representation of something else, e.g., the structure of thoughts or of independently given facts. Since language is autonomous, it is a cardinal mistake to try to explain features of its structure in terms of features of other structures. This kind of mistake, Saussure thought, is all too prevalent, and is one which philosophers of language are especially prone to make.

In an interesting passage at the beginning of Part 1, Chapter 1, of *CLG* Saussure criticises the view that language is essentially a nomenclature, i.e., the view that words are simply labels of independently identifiable things:

> This conception is open to criticism at several points. It assumes that ready-made ideas exist before words...; it does not tell whether a name is vocal or psychological in nature (*arbor*, for instance, can be considered from either viewpoint); finally it lets us assume that the linking of a name and a thing is a very simple operation – an assumption that is anything but true. (*CLG*, 97, 65)

To be sure, the points are made so briefly that it is difficult to be certain what weight to attach to them. So it is an important point that this is in fact a very condensed version of a note in Saussure's own hand addressed specifically to philosophers (Engler 2, 147F).

Most thinkers about language, he argues in this note, approach it as though it were a nomenclature. The majority of philosophical conceptions make one think of Adam calling the animals before him and giving them names. But the conception of language as a nomenclature has three grave defects. To begin with,

> the basis of language is not constituted by names. It is an accident when a linguistic sign is found to correspond to a perceptual object, such as *a horse, the fire, the sun*, <rather than an idea such as *'il posa'*>. Whatever is the importance of this case there is no evident reason to take it as typical of language. (Engler 2, 148F)

But not only does the nomenclaturist view of language go astray because most words are not names and do not designate things, it also assumes that there exists

> *first* the object, then the sign; therefore (what we always deny), that there is an external basis to the sign, and that language can be represented as follows:

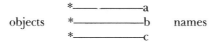

although the true representation is

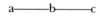

apart from all <knowledge of an effective relation, such as
*——a based on an object>. (Ibid.)

In other words, nomenclaturism goes astray not simply because
most signs are not names, but more fundamentally because its
account of the significance of a sign is not intralinguistic, that is
in terms of its relations to other signs, but extralinguistic, in
terms of its relation to something independently identifiable. In
giving this kind of account, nomenclaturism impugns the autonomy of language. In the passage cited, the external objects
in question are perceptual ones; however, Saussure makes it clear
that he is resolutely opposed to the idea that signs have an external basis of any kind. So he objected just as strongly to the
kind of determination of signs by 'elements' of thoughts envisaged by the *Port Royal Grammar*.

A third mistake which Saussure thought nomenclaturism
made was that it totally ignored the effect of time. For the
changes wrought by time affect not only the words used to designate a thing or idea – e.g., the Latin *calidum* becomes the French
chaud (warm) – but also the very ideas they express – e.g., the
Latin *crimen* (accusation) becomes our 'crime'. But if nomenclaturism were correct and words were merely labels for independently identifiable things, then, Saussure thought, this should
not happen; only the words (= labels) should change (Amacker
1975, 83).

As they stand, the arguments are too abbreviated to make
serious evaluation profitable; the third, for instance, seems to be
an objection to a Platonistic version of nomenclaturism which
few would espouse. But there is no doubt that the first two
arguments sketched here are ones which Saussure reverts to time
and time again, amplifying them at many points, when discussing
the principle of the Arbitrariness of the Sign and its ramifications
(3.2). The third argument is developed in great detail in his
discussion of linguistic change (Chapter 4) and indeed seems to
be involved in a separate if little-noticed argument for the arbitrariness of the sign.[4]

Thus, not only did Saussure dissociate himself very sharply
indeed from nomenclaturism, but he also believed that the traditional grammar had not freed itself from this conception, since

it tried to base itself on something 'given'. Moreover, in so doing it impugned the autonomy of language, as did all other theories which tried to explain features of signs in terms of the features of independently identifiable extralinguistic entities. Evidently a radically new approach was called for.

1.3. The writing of *CLG*

In their introduction to *CLG* the editors explain the problem they had in preparing the text. When Saussure died in 1913 they had hoped to find extensive notes used by him for the courses in general linguistics that he gave in 1907, 1908–9, and 1910–11 – his only lectures on this topic. But they were disappointed, finding 'nothing – or almost nothing – that resembled his students' notebooks' (*CLG*, 7, xxix). Moreover, they had not attended his lectures themselves – if they had, their expectation of finding extensive notes might well have been different, since it seems that often Saussure came armed with no more than little pieces of paper. However, though the lectures were attended by relatively few students, they had kept unusually detailed notes. Four students supplied the editors with their notes of the first two courses, and three with their notes for the third course. These notes, together with some additional material, provided the editors with a different problem from that arising from the absence of Saussure's own notes, for there was if anything almost too much material. The notes of Riedlinger, for instance, their only source for the First Course as well as the most detailed for the Second Course, total 732 pages. As they say, 'to publish everything in the original form was impossible' (*CLG*, 8, xxx).

After considering a number of alternatives, they decided to take the Third Course as their starting point,

> using all the other materials at our disposal, including the personal notes of F. de Saussure, as supplementary sources. . . . At each point we had to get to the crux of each particular thought by trying to see its definitive form in the light of the whole system. We had first to weed out variations and irregularities characteristic of oral delivery, then to fit the thought into its natural framework and present each part of it in the order intended by the author even when his intention, not always apparent, had to be surmised. (*CLG*, 9, xxxi)

However, the impression left by this, that though the text of *CLG* is not Saussure's its relation to the surviving records of his teaching is relatively straightforward, is very misleading. For publication of Godel's *Les sources manuscrites du cours de linguistique générale* in 1957 and of Engler's critical edition of *CLG* in 1967 makes it clear just how bold the work of the editors had been, so much so that one commentator, Calvet, has argued that the resulting text gives a completely misleading impression of Saussure's project (1975, 54).

The editors' initiatives are grouped by Calvet under three headings. The first of these, unsurprisingly, raises questions about the heterogeneity of their sources and the way in which they have amalgamated them. A good example of this sort of difficulty would be Part 1, Chapter 1, of *CLG*, which is based on the notes of four students as well as on a long manuscript note of Saussure's. The editors' task was complicated by the fact that, having had second thoughts about the order of presentation, Saussure proposed a new title for the chapter in question, namely 'La langue comme système de signes' and also the replacement of a pair of contrasting terms which he had originally used, 'acoustic image' and 'concept', by the terms *signifiant* (signifier) and *signifié* (signified) (3.1.1). So as well as having to decide how to incorporate four different sources into a unitary text, the editors also had to decide both whether to adopt the new suggestion for a chapter heading, which oddly enough they did not do, and how to replace the terms 'acoustic image' and 'concept' with the proposed terms. It is therefore far from surprising that, as de Mauro points out, the resulting text is a mixture of the two terminologies, and by no means always a happy one[5] (*TM*, 439).

The second type of editorial initiative involves adding material of their own to which nothing in the sources seems to correspond. It is perhaps surprising, but there seem to be sentences in the text which have no known analogues in the published sources. These include the famous closing remark:

> From the incursions we have made into the borderlands of our science, one lesson stands out. It is wholly negative, but it is the more interesting because it agrees with the fundamental idea of

this course: *the true and unique object of linguistics is language (la langue) studied in and for itself.* (*CLG*, 317, 232)

Doubtless nearly every sentence of their text presented the editors with delicate decisions. They surely had at times to make additions to make explicit what was implicit in the sources, or to amalgamate them into a coherent text (*TM*, 407). Moreover, they were right to do so in the light of an overall interpretation of Saussure's thought. But it was surely quite another matter to incorporate into the text summaries of that interpretation, however justified the summary may have been. Normal editorial practice would be to include such summaries in a preface or in footnotes flagged 'Eds.'

Moreover, as de Mauro points out, this particular interpretation was at the same time both highly tendentious and influential (*TM,* 476). To be sure, one could argue that it is not without warrant, citing the famous passage *'from the very outset we must put both feet on the ground of language (la langue) and use language as the norm of all other manifestations of speech (langage)'* (*CLG*, 25, 9). But even if this passage were itself unproblematical, which it is not,[6] it is quite different to argue that a study of *la langue* should form the basis of all studies of language, whether they be comparativist, geographical, or something else, than it is to argue that language (*la langue*) should be studied for its own sake. On either account a study of *la langue* is central, but whereas the first account does not deny the existence of other legitimate points of view from which language can be studied, the second does.

The third type of editorial initiative raises questions about the overall structure of *CLG*. Here the real burden of complaint against the editors is not that they changed the order of the Third Course; it is rather that though they leave the impression that it has been observed and that material from elsewhere has been used only to supplement it, in fact they depart from it at many points. Consulting *SM* shows that *CLG* makes use of material from all three of the courses, presenting it in an order which follows none of them very closely (*SM*, 103).

In fact, as Calvet points out, broadly speaking the actual order the editors adopted inverts that of the Third Course. After a preliminary lecture devoted to the history of linguistics and a discussion of the object of linguistics, Saussure's next lecture outlines the overall structure of his course:

> November 4th. General division of the course:
> 1. *Languages.* (*Les langues.*)
> 2. *Language.* (*La langue.*)
> 3. The language faculty (*langage*) and its exercise by individuals.
>
> Justification of this order: the difficulty of determining the concrete object of linguistics. To begin with, it is necessary to separate from the faculty of language (*langage*) *language* itself (*la langue*), a social product, a semiological institution: There is the object of linguistics. But this social product manifests itself through a great variety of languages. It is therefore necessary to begin with what is given: languages; then to extract what is universal: *la langue*. Only then will one concern oneself with the individual's use of language. (*SM*, 77)[7]

But whereas the Third Course begins with extensive reflections on the plurality of languages, geographical diversity and its causes, and so on, *CLG* relegates nearly all of this material to Part 4, a part which many who have read the book to see what Saussure has to say about synchronic linguistics will at best have skimmed; yet, except for an interlude for a discussion of phonology, this material took up Saussure's lectures from 4 November 1910 to 25 April 1911. Furthermore, even if one confines oneself to sections dealing only with synchronic issues, there are unexplained departures from the Third Course.[8]

Further discussion of textual issues would be out of place here. But this brief survey shows that, at the very least, great caution is needed when citing the text of *CLG* as evidence of Saussure's views.[9]

1.4. Summary and prospect

By training a comparative linguist, Saussure became dissatisfied with the theoretical and methodological assumptions underlying the practice of the field (1.1). Though he never doubted that it was legitimate to attempt to describe the evolution and development of particular languages, and in so doing relate them to other languages, he believed that comparative linguists were always in danger of going seriously astray because of their failure to ask fundamental questions, in particular what precisely is being compared with what. This brings up a fundamental question: What are the units to be studied and what are their identity conditions?

Thus Saussure's dissatisfaction with historical linguistics led to a concerted effort to answer the question 'What is the object of linguistics?' – undoubtedly the central question addressed in *CLG*. Moreover, his answer to it is a striking reversal of the intellectual perspective in which he had grown up, since he claims that the primary study is a descriptive one of the state of a language at a given time, a *synchronic* study, rather than a study of the changes undergone by a language through time, a *diachronic* study. Now that his views on this matter have become the norm, it is difficult to appreciate how both novel and revolutionary his position was, yet it unquestionably represented a major shift in perspective, however incompletely it may have been worked out in detail.

The question of the object of linguistics was central in another respect. For in the course of expanding his answers Saussure developed a conception of language as a social institution in conscious opposition to the organicist conceptions of it to which he objected so vehemently (1.1). This conception stresses the autonomy of language; that is, maintains that the forms of possible linguistic representations are not constrained by anything external or prior. Clearly the *Port Royal Grammar* did not acknowledge the autonomy of language (1.2), since though language is, according to it, structured, its structure is a reflection of something else: thought. Moreover, the characteristic failing of philosophical approaches to language is nomenclaturism, the assumption that words serve simply as labels for independently identifiable things (1.2). But since, as Saussure saw, it is difficult to avoid some form of nomenclaturism, the rejection of any form of it is a radical move, calling for the development of a very different conception of language than that customarily held.

If the conception of a language as an autonomous social institution, *sui generis* precisely because it is autonomous, was a second radical idea that Saussure grappled with in *CLG*, there is arguably a third, namely that of the study of language as part of a more general study of sign systems, semiology. But though this idea has been extremely important for the development of structuralism, it is not obviously consistent with the idea of a language as an autonomous social institution. Since semiology as such did not exist when Saussure wrote, this tension might not seem to matter, since it could be argued that little is lost in the development of Saussure's system by giving up the semiological approach. I shall discuss this response later in more detail (7.4); but for the time being it may stand provisionally, since it is clear that a considerable part of Saussure's argument does not depend essentially on adopting a semiological approach.

The ways in which Saussure attempts to develop these themes in detail, and the problems that arise in doing so, form the substance of the remainder of the book. We begin in the next chapter, as Saussure did, with a discussion of the central question: What is the object of linguistics?

—⫷ ⫸—

2

THE DISTINCTION BETWEEN
LANGUE AND *PAROLE*

As Saussure himself did, I begin the systematic exposition of his views with the distinction between *langue* and *parole*. But why begin here? One reason is the unquestionable importance of the distinction for Saussure's system. However, given his overall semiological approach (7.4), the question arises whether the distinction could in fact be derived from some fundamental principles of semiology, in which case it would be natural to begin with them. This is a difficult question, which will be discussed in Chapter 7, where it will be argued that there is no convincing derivation of this kind, so that there is no alternative to treating it as an independent distinction.[1]

The overall aim of Chapter 3 of the Introduction to *CLG* is to answer the question 'What is both the integral and concrete object of linguistics?' (*CLG*, 23, 7), so a major part of Saussure's interest in drawing the distinction is to enable him to give a precise answer to that question. Moreover, it is clear that the concept of *langue* plays a crucial role in the answer he gives. What is disputable is not this, but the nature of that role. Is *langue* itself definitive of the object, so that linguistics is confined to a study of it and nothing else? Or is it that without which we cannot define an object of study, which includes *langue* of course, but other things as well?[2] I shall argue that the second of these

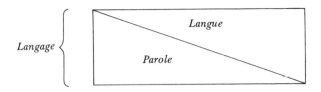

Figure 2.1

alternatives was the one Saussure maintained, whereas the famous final remarks of *CLG*, which we saw are the editors' and not Saussure's, attribute the first view to him (1.3).

One final comment. Though the subject matter of this chapter is a dichotomy, in fact three terms are being distinguished, namely natural language – *langage*; a particular language – *langue*; and speech – *parole*.[3] Indeed, Saussure spends if anything more time trying to distinguish *langue* from *langage* than he does trying to distinguish it from *parole*. Unfortunately, the distinctions Saussure is trying to make in French are far from easy to express in English, so I shall continue in this section to try to express Saussure's thoughts as naturally as I can, whilst at the same time citing the corresponding French terms.[4]

2.1. The nature of the distinction

How then are language (*langue*) and speech (*parole*) related to each other, and both to natural language (*langage*)? The central idea seems to be that the latter can be divided exhaustively into two sub-domains, namely language and speech. Following Godel, this relation can be represented as in Figure 2.1 (1957, 153). If we think of this as a semiological definition, then *langue* and *parole* are being explained in terms of their relations with each other, by means of a set of contrasts:

Langue	*Parole*
Social	Individual
Essential	Contingent
No active individual role	Active role
Not designed	Designed

Conventional	Not conventional
Furnishes a homogeneous subject matter for a branch of social psychology	Furnishes a heterogeneous subject matter studied by different disciplines

More will be said in the next section about each of these contrasts and Saussure's reasons for making it, together with the distinction it underpins.

2.1.1. The basis of the distinction

Saussure's argument begins by considering the view that linguistics should concern itself just with sounds. If someone utters the French word *nu*, are we not presented with a concrete object that can be studied?

Saussure's response to this suggestion is that whether we are considering a sound, a word, or something else depends on what *kind* of thing we have in mind: Is it a sound, the expression of an idea, an equivalent of the Latin *nudum*? (*CLG*, 23, 8). But in the latter two cases, in which what we are considering is indeed a linguistic item, we have to consider it not simply as a sound but as an instantiation of an element of a language. So to consider an utterance of *nu* as one of a word is not to consider it as a purely physical event, in the way in which one might consider 'Ah' uttered by someone as purely an involuntary exclamation. The sounds we make when speaking, considered just as sounds, can be described by someone who does not know to which language they belong. To describe them as words, one must know what features of them are functionally significant from the point of view of the language to which they belong.[5]

Perhaps the best way to convince oneself of the importance of linguistic knowledge for the identification of a word is to note that someone who does not speak English will hear the sequence of sounds [passthesugar] as a continuous sequence in which there are no natural divisions, whereas an English speaker will hear it as a three-word sentence, 'Pass the sugar.' Knowledge of English enables him or her to segment the sequence into three meaning-bearing units, which it is impossible to do without such knowledge.[6] It is, I think, this point that Saussure is making when he writes:

But suppose that sound were a simple thing: would it constitute speech (*langage*)? No, it is only an instrument of thought; by itself it has no existence. At this point a new and redoubtable relationship arises: a sound, a complex acoustical–vocal unit, combines in turn with an idea to form a complex physiological–psychological unit. (*CLG*, 24, 8)

In other words, since sound is only the instrument of thought, the sorts of sounds linguistics is interested in are not simply sounds, but sounds that have meaning, or functionally significant units of such sounds.

The issue raised in this passage – what is involved in the identification of a word – is for Saussure an absolutely central question. Failure to realise its importance and to answer it satisfactorily lay, he believed, at the root of the confusions of comparative linguistics, and it is a question to which he returns repeatedly in *CLG* (1.1). The answer he gives at this point, that a word cannot be identified with a sound as such but has to be considered as a meaning-bearing item, is, of course, only a preliminary answer; but the negative thesis that linguistics is not concerned with sounds qua sounds is one that stands without further qualification.

Before proposing his alternative to the view that language is constituted by sounds, Saussure makes two claims about natural language (*langage*) which it is essential to keep in mind. First, it has both a 'social and an individual side'; and second, it 'always implies both an established system and an evolution; at every moment it is both an existing institution and a product of the past' (*CLG*, 24, 8).

But if we must take all of these factors into consideration, the search for the object of linguistics is made even harder:

... if we fix our attention on only one side of each problem, we run the risk of failing to perceive the dualities pointed out above; on the other hand, if we study speech (*langage*) from several viewpoints simultaneously, the object of linguistics appears to us as a confused mass of heterogeneous and unrelated things. (*CLG*, 24, 9)

In other words, to concentrate on just one aspect, e.g., the social, would be to ignore the others, the individual, the institutional, and the evolutionary; whilst to study all aspects simultaneously would leave no unifying core.

Saussure's solution to this dilemma is bold. It is to award *langue* the pre-eminent place in the study of natural language (*langage*), subordinating the other studiable aspects to it. It can be awarded this place, Saussure argues, for a number of reasons: It admits of an independent definition; it is a self-contained whole; and it is a principle of classification (*CLG*, 25, 9). This last claim is puzzling if taken to mean that *langue* itself provides a principle for classifying the other aspects of natural language. But what I suggest it means is not that, but rather that it provides a principle for classifying linguistic units, such as *nu*.[7] This would indeed be a reason for awarding it a pre-eminent place and for subordinating other studies to it if, as seems plausible, they had to presuppose the results of such classifications. An interest in speech acts, for instance, might lead one to note that the choice between 'you' and 'I' as agent in the schema '——will go' can make the difference between a directive and a commissive interpretation, e.g., between a request and a promise. But such an observation obviously assumes that we already know how to analyse sentences structurally.

But what is *langue*? At this stage Saussure's characterisation is tantalisingly brief:

> It is not to be confused with human speech [*langage*], of which it is only a definite part, though certainly an essential one. It is both a social product of the faculty of speech and a collection of necessary conventions that have been adopted by a social body to permit individuals to exercise that faculty. (*CLG*, 25, 9)

His response to an imagined objection explains in part what he means. The objection is that, after all, when we speak we make use of a natural faculty, our vocal apparatus, whereas *langue* is constituted by convention. To this he replies that whilst Whitney may well have gone too far in arguing that we might just as well have used gestures and visual symbols rather than acoustical ones, he is right to insist that the actual nature of the sign is a matter of secondary importance. Appealing to a definition of 'articulated speech' as the subdivision of a chain of meanings into significant units, he argues that what is natural to man is not 'oral speech but the faculty of constructing a language' (*CLG*, 26, 10). Presumably he thinks that, by comparison, the study of the means used to articulate a language is of importance secondary to a study of the language itself. For he goes on to adduce findings of Broca which, he argues, show that various oral disorders are attributable not to the malfunctioning of specific organs, but to the malfunction of a general faculty, so that they affect writing as well:[8] 'The obvious implication is that beyond the functioning of the various organs there exists a more general faculty which governs signs and which would be the linguistic faculty proper' (*CLG*, 27, 11). So what we should be interested in is the nature of the underlying faculty rather than any one of the particular instruments, such as speech used to articulate it.

But how does this faculty relate to *langue*? It is surely not clear that *langue* can be identified with the faculty of language, since what is common to people who speak different languages is the possession of that faculty. But if it cannot be so identified, then the question arises whether the object of our study should be the latter rather than the former. I shall discuss later what Saussure's answer to this objection might have been (2.3). However, a hint of an answer is contained in his final argument for giving a pre-eminent place to *langue*, namely that 'the faculty of articulating words – whether it is natural or not – is exercised only with the help of an instrument created by a collectivity and provided for its use; therefore to say that language (*langue*) gives unity to speech (*langage*) is not fanciful' (*CLG*, 27, 11). In other words, without a language (*langue*), which is a social product, the faculty can do nothing.

2.1.2. *The model of communication*

These arguments for distinguishing *langue* from natural language (*langage*) tell us neither how to relate the two nor how to relate *langue* to what is left of *langage* when *langue* is, as it were, subtracted from it. It is these questions which are addressed next; perhaps surprisingly, a certain model of communication plays an important role in Saussure's argument at this point. I say surprisingly, because Saussure never explains why this model is the appropriate one, but simply introduces it without further justification.

This is an important point, because it seems that there are a number of assumptions implicit in the choice of this model which

Figure 2.2

are central to his argument. The first of these is that language is an instrument of which the primary use is in communication (Ducrot 1968, 66; Aarsleff 1967). The second is that face-to-face oral communication is the relevant norm (Harris 1987, 25). It might indeed be said that the second assumption is reasonable if his arguments that writing is a secondary, parasitic system go through (2.2.1); though this would still leave the question of what linguistics has to say about such secondary systems. But, as far as I can see, the first assumption, if it is indeed one that Saussure makes, is entirely unsupported.

Saussure's model assumes that a typical communicative exchange involves two people in face-to-face contact talking to each other (fig. 2.2). Let us suppose that they engage in a simple exchange:

(1) A: Do you have the time?
    B: Six-thirty.

Precisely how is this to be described in detail? Saussure postulates a place (module?) in A's brain (*sic*) 'where mental facts (concepts) are associated with representations of the linguistic sounds (sound images) that are used for their expression' (*CLG*, 28, 11). So, for example, the concept of a cat is associated with a representation of the sound one hears when the word 'cat' is pronounced.

When A speaks, the following things happen:

(i) A concept (or concepts) in A's head unlocks the corresponding sound image(s). This is a psychological process.
(ii) The brain transmits an impulse corresponding to the sound image to the organs producing the sounds.

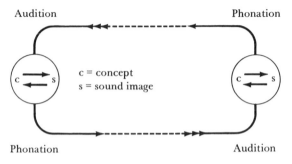

Figure 2.3

(iii) Sound waves travel to B's ear: a purely physical process.
(iv) These now activate a sound image in B's brain: a process
       which Saussure describes as physiological, so presumably
       (ii) is also.
 (v) The sound image now unlocks the corresponding concept
       in B's brain: another purely psychological process.

All of this constitutes one-half of a circuit, which is completed
when B goes on to say something. The completion of the overall
exchange is illustrated by Saussure in Figure 2.3. Saussure points
out that this circuit could be complicated, but argues that the
simple diagram includes everything essential.[9] But where in all
of this are we to locate *langue*?

Saussure's answer seems to depend on three distinctions.
The first is between, on the one hand, what is psychological,
namely the associative relations between concepts and sound
images, and, on the other, everything else, that is the physiological and physical processes. The second is between, on
the one hand, what is active, namely everything involved
in (i), (ii), and (iii), and, on the other, what is passive, that is
everything involved in (iv) and (v).[10] Finally, Saussure distinguishes between what is executive (i) and what is receptive (v).

At this point Saussure's argument becomes very difficult to
follow. This is in part because the text makes it natural to assume
that he is trying to locate a place for *langue* somewhere in the
circuit, despite the fact that if he was it would be very difficult
to make sense of the claim that *langue* is social. In fact what he
is doing is quite different, namely trying to explain how it comes

about that each member of a linguistic community has a similar representation of its *langue*.

His argument seems to be this: So far, our account has been too simple in that it has omitted the 'associative and coordinating faculty . . . [which] plays the dominant role in the organization of language as a system' (*CLG*, 29, 13). Roughly speaking, this faculty relates individual signs to other signs.[11] Now, to understand the role of this faculty we have to consider social facts. For when a group of individuals converse with each other 'all will reproduce – not exactly of course, but approximately – the same signs united with the same concepts' (ibid.). If this happens – and Saussure of course simply asserts that it does – then the social fact in question to be accounted for is the fact that the members of the linguistic community in question do this.

Now, some parts of the circuit that we have been considering cannot be responsible. The non-psychological part can be ruled out for a start. For, to repeat the argument about *nu* considered earlier, 'when we hear people speaking a language we do not know, we perceive the sounds but remain outside the social fact because we do not understand them' (ibid.). But neither is the psychological part wholly responsible. The executive side is always individual, by which I take Saussure to mean that the speaker chooses what to say. So all that is left is the receptive side, and it is through this that 'impressions that are perceptibly the same for all are made in the minds of speakers' (ibid.). We can picture this social product, their common language, as

> a storehouse filled by the members of a given community through their active use of speaking (*parole*), a grammatical system that has potential existence in each brain, or more specifically in the brains of a group of individuals. For language is not complete in any speaker; it exists perfectly only within a collectivity. (Ibid.)

So, charitably interpreted, Saussure is claiming that *langue* is social because it is the product of face-to-face communicative interchanges between members of a linguistic community, each of whom, as a result of these interchanges, has a similar representation of it. This accounts for the way in which a sort of average is set up among the members of a community; moreover, it requires us to treat the existence of the *langue* of a community as something that has to be explained as the product of communicative exchanges between individuals. Further, on this account, at any given time the fundamental psychological reality is the existence of separate but similar representations of their *langue* in the brains of the members of the community. What makes their collective existence a social fact is simply the explanation of how those representations are acquired, why they are similar, and the role they play in face-to-face communication. There is no need to invoke the idea of a collective mind and its representations, unless indeed this is simply a shorthand way of talking about the representations in the minds of individuals within the community; in other words, there is no need to posit a supra-individual collective mind.

However, it has been argued that the image of the storehouse suggests that as well as this 'average' conception of *langue*, which only requires members of the linguistic community to have similar representations of their language, Saussure also entertained a different one, which does reify *langue*, treating it as something independent of individual representations of it, having a potential existence in the minds of individuals but existing perfectly only in the collectivity.

Now, whether the passage in which the image of the storehouse is introduced does commit Saussure to reifying *langue* seems to me to be a moot point, though it is often taken to do so (cf. Harris 1987, 199). Saussure does not say that a language exists independently of all members of the linguistic community; merely that it only exists perfectly within a collectivity. This might only be a rather clumsy way of trying to deal with the fact that, for instance, different speakers have different vocabularies, so that if we wanted to construct a dictionary of their language the result would involve idealisation in that it would include all the items that any member of the community might use, even though no one member would use all of them. Such idealisation would seem to be not only harmless but essential for any serious study.

It would, of course, also be true on the average conception that a given *langue* is not dependent for its existence on any particular member of the community. Elsewhere Saussure repeatedly stresses the need for a community and the powerlessness of any individual on his own to modify *langue*; but, correct or not, these points require no more than the 'average' conception.

A possible source of confusion in Saussure's position might be traced to his psychologism. The average conception calls for a distinction between elements of a language, e.g., words and parts of speech, and individual representations of them. But for Saussure the elements of language are psychological entities, housed in the brain, which makes it difficult, though perhaps not impossible, to make such a distinction. So it would perhaps be easy to conclude that if the language is incomplete in an individual, the remainder has to be somewhere else.

There is indeed one passage which might be cited to prove that Saussure was committed to the reification of *langue*. In this passage he points out that we can assimilate the linguistic systems of dead languages to illustrate his claim that we can study *langue* without studying its use in speech. However, this claim threatens to undermine several of his key assumptions. Presumably this assimilation is done on the basis of written records and without face-to-face contact, a point which raises issues that I shall discuss a little later (2.2.1).

Whether or not Saussure is committed to anything more than the average conception is, of course, a key issue, to which we shall have to return (7.3); but as an interim conclusion I would urge that he is not, that the argument considered does no more than explain how different speakers come to have roughly similar representations of their *langue*, and that what makes the existence of a *langue* a social fact is the explanation of the way it is acquired by individuals and the role that their representations of it play in each interpreting the other's speech.

As for Saussure's claim that language is passive, it is clear that it is really a claim about how it is learned. The individual who assimilates it by participating in communicative interchanges plays no active part in its assimilation. This is an important point from his perspective. For if the individual did contribute something to the acquisition of a language, then the possibility would arise that factors other than the purely communicative–social ones, which are of crucial importance according to him, come into play.

So it is important to note that the argument adduced by appeal to the speech-circuit model is quite inadequate to show that an individual plays no active part in the assimilation of his or her language. Even if it is true that an acoustic image automatically unlocks its corresponding concept, that is true only of someone like B who has already learnt the language and for whom the relevant associations have been established, whereas to prove his

point, Saussure has to show that B played no active part in
acquiring those associations. And even if it is true, as Saussure
claims, that no individual can alone change the language which
he or she speaks, this goes no way to showing that acquisition
of it is a purely passive process.

Other aspects of Saussure's theory of language require discussion, in particular his claim that it is a well-defined object.
But first I must say something about the other term of the dichotomy, *parole*.

2.1.3. Speech

It may seem odd that the discussion of the distinction between
langue and *parole* has taken so long to introduce the latter term,
but in this respect it is not unfaithful to Saussure's own discussion. It is only in the course of the explanation of how it is that
the average conception of *langue* is crystallised in the brains of
members of the community that the term is introduced, almost
as an aside. After arguing that the psychological part of the
circuit is not wholly responsible for the crystallisation of language, and that the executive component must be excluded, he
adds: 'Execution is always individual, and the individual is always
its master: I shall call the executive side *speaking* (*parole*)' (*CLG*,
30, 13). This suggests, given the explanation of 'executive', that
the domain of speech is to be restricted to what goes on when
an acoustic image is associated with a concept, but that does not
seem to be Saussure's real view. For a little later he attributes a
much wider domain to it: 'Within the act, we should distinguish
between: (1) the combinations by which the speaker uses the
language code for expressing his own thought: and (2) the psy-
chophysical mechanism that allows him to exteriorize those combinations' (*CLG*, 31, 14). The students' notes make it clear that
by the former Saussure had in mind an individual's use of the
linguistic code to express thought, and by the latter everything
involved in speech production, including phonation. In other
words, the linguistics of *parole* has as its subject matter everything
in the speech circuit that is not passive; it is hardly surprising
that, if this is how it is conceived, it is heterogeneous in the
extreme.

Indeed, the subject matter of *parole* is even more extensive
than it seems at first sight. The brief passage on the subject gives

no idea of the extent envisaged by Saussure of the indiv
freedom when making use of a linguistic code to express
thought. It is not simply a matter of a choice between alternative
formulations of what is intuitively the same thought, such as that
between:

(2a) John kissed Mary in the garden

and

(2b) It was in the garden that John kissed Mary

in response to the questions

(3a) What did John do?

and

(3b) What happened in the garden?

The kind of freedom envisaged by Saussure is much more extensive than this, in that he seems to have seen the generation
of the sentences themselves as something which is not part of
langue but something done by individual speakers; note the sentence 'belongs to speaking (*parole*), and not to language (*langue*)'
(*CLG*, 172, 124).[12] Thus Saussure apparently excludes from the
object of linguistics, *langue*, much that modern linguistics would
include, so that its domain is extremely limited. Chomsky
comments:

> He was thus quite unable to come to grips with the recursive
> processes underlying sentence formation, and he appears to re-
> gard sentence formation as a matter of *parole* rather than *langue*,
> of free and voluntary creation rather than systematic rule. There
> is no place in his scheme for 'rule-governed creativity' of the kind
> involved in the ordinary everyday use of language. (1964, 23)

By contrast, the domain of *parole*, everything to do with *langage*
that remains when *langue* has been subtracted, is positively vast.
But though it is clear that it is vast, it is far from clear precisely
what its extent is, because it is not clear what should be included

in the domain of facts belonging to *langage*. If that were clear, then provided it was also clear which subset of facts belonged to *langue*, it would be clear what is encompassed by *parole* – the facts that are left when those belonging to *langue* are subtracted from those belonging to *langage*. However, we cannot tell from Saussure's schematic representation of the speech circuit, which leaves various kinds of linguistic fact unrepresented, just how many relevant linguistic facts are in fact unrepresented on it. For instance, those considerations relevant to the determination of A's speech act in (1) as a request and B's as a reply are omitted, even though B's response takes the precise form it does only because A's remarks are recognised as a request. It is difficult to avoid the conclusion that not only is the term *parole* not well defined, but that it is hard to see how it could be. Given the vagueness of the term 'linguistic fact', it is simply unclear what the remainder is when we try to subtract *langue* from *langage* (cf. fig. 2.1).

Since *parole* is on this account such a rag-bag, corresponding to no natural category, the description of it as heterogeneous is, as I said, hardly surprising. However, the proper response to this is surely that what is called for is not concentration on the allegedly well-defined object *langue* to the exclusion of everything else, but an attempt to distinguish well-defined areas within this heterogeneous domain. For example, Saussure treats what he calls phonology, the study of the articulatory and acoustic properties of speech, as 'an auxiliary discipline which belongs to *parole*' (*CLG*, 55, 33).[13] That is, he tries to isolate a particular area of *parole* about which he thinks it is possible to say something systematic, particularly at the level of combinatory phonology – the study of the constraints which the articulation of one speech sound places on succeeding ones (*CLG*, 79, 51). Of course, he may have been mistaken in supposing that there is anything systematic to be said on this subject, but he was surely right to try to isolate one or more areas of *parole* for systematic study.

The crucial question, then, seems to be not how we rigorously define *parole*, for that is an enquiry which can lead nowhere, but rather what explanatory functions *parole* has in Saussure's system, and which areas within the heterogeneous domain need to be isolated for purposes of these explanations. There seem to be three such functions. First, *parole* is needed, as we saw, to explain how the social crytallisation of *langue* occurs. What is in question in this case are those systematic features of language *use* which make face-to-face communication possible. Second, *parole* is needed to explain how the speaker constructs a sentence; this is a matter of his or her free choice of elements belonging to *langue*. Third, as we shall see (4.5), Saussure appeals to *parole* to explain how languages change: 'It is in speaking that the germ of all change is found. Each change is launched by a certain number of individuals before it is accepted for general use' (*CLG*, 138, 98). Thus *parole* is needed to explain not only how *langue* is constituted as a stable system in a community, but also how changes occur in it.

Now, precisely what theories are needed to perform these functions is not a question that we can answer here – though, as we have just seen, many would argue that the second is performed by an enriched concept of *langue* which includes syntax. But it is at least clear in outline that in the first case a detailed explanation would have to draw on a theory of the articulation and perception of speech sounds and of their functionally significant features, that is on phonetics and phonology as well as a theory of the constitutive features of speech acts. Whether these could all be regarded as disciplines auxiliary to a study of *langue* is a separate issue. But it is surely clear that instead of continuing to talk about *parole* as an undifferentiated whole opposed to *langue*, conceptual clarity requires that one attempt to isolate areas of study within that whole and investigate their dependence on the study of *langue*. Nor does it seem that Saussure could object to this – nor indeed would have, given his treatment of phonetics (what he calls phonology) as an auxiliary science, since it is only when this has been done that the metaphor of *langue* as the platform on which everything else rests can be cashed in. Indeed, he says as much:

> In granting the science of language (*langue*) its correct place within the overall study of speech (*langage*), I have at the same time located linguistics itself. All other elements of speech – those that constitute speaking (*parole*) – freely subordinate themselves to the first science, and it is by virtue of this subordination that the parts of linguistics find their natural place. (*CLG*, 36, 17)

It is true that the degree of subordination envisaged by him is at times considerable. Language is likened to a symphony, which exists independently of any of its performances; mistakes, if there are any, are the fault of the musicians and not defects in the symphony. The vocal apparatus itself is likened to a device used to transmit Morse Code, that is to something of no intrinsic interest in relation to the code, which could be transmitted in many other ways.

This last analogy, indeed, suggests that strictly speaking the nature of the instrument is of no interest at all. But that would not be true of the first. Symphonies are written for specific instruments and contain detailed instructions for their use. Which analogy is followed obviously makes a difference; as we shall see, Saussure follows sometimes one, sometimes the other.

On this account of the Saussurean programme, it is clear why the study of *langue* should be viewed as pre-eminent. It is because in a quite literal sense it is what gives unity to the study of language (*langage*); and because this is so, other areas of study, those belonging to *parole*, are subordinate to it. This account is, of course, quite different from one that advocates concentration on the study of *langue* 'in and for itself', as did the editors in the last sentence of *CLG*, at least if this is interpreted as a warrant to ignore the diverse studies belonging to the field of *parole* (*TM*, 476). Moreover, it should be clear that anyone who took this advice would be in the position of someone who had climbed a ladder and then thrown it away. The concept of *parole* is essential for Saussure's general theory of language, as is evident from the list of explanatory functions considered above.

Earlier in the discussion Saussure pointed out that language (*langage*) has both a social and an individual aspect. It should now be clear in what respects he thinks it social and in what respects not; everything pertaining to *langue* is social, whereas *parole* is individual.

2.1.4. Langue *as a self-contained object*

Of course *langue* could only have the pre-eminent position Saussure gives it if it is indeed a self-contained object capable of an independent definition (cf. 2.1). But why did he think it was? The first reason he gives seems less than convincing: 'It can be localized in the limited segment of the speaking-circuit where an auditory image becomes associated with a concept' (*CLG*, 31, 14). For there are a variety of respects in which this is not self-contained; acoustic images, for instance, are causally related to other parts of the circuit. Nor is the fact that we are dealing with the social side of speech – something institutional existing 'only by virtue of a sort of contract signed by members of the community' (ibid.) – a guarantee of the requisite sort of independence, for many institutions are constrained by external factors. If it is an institution, it will have to be one of a very special sort to constitute a self-contained object, which indeed Saussure thinks it is: 'Several features set it apart from other political, legal, etc. institutions' (*CLG*, 33, 15).

What makes language special, he argues, is that it is a semiological system comparable to other systems of this sort, such as writing, Morse Code, and the sign language of the deaf (7.4). But though comparable it is the most important of such systems:

> Linguistics is only a part of the general science of semiology; the laws discovered by semiology will be applicable to linguistics, and the latter will circumscribe a well-defined area within the mass of anthropological facts.... The task of the linguist is to find out what makes a language a special system within the mass of semiological data. (*CLG*, 33, 16)

Since the science of semiology did not exist, Saussure's move at this point is, to say the least, surprising. There were no known semiological laws, so there was precisely nothing to appeal to. Moreover, the history of semiology since Saussure's time does not inspire confidence that there are any discoverable laws at all (7.4).

However, what Saussure is proposing is, I suggest, more modest. Granted that there were no known semiological laws to appeal to, it would still be possible to make a start on the development of semiology by asking what is special about linguistic signs, investigating the ways in which they form systems, and whenever possible making comparisons with other sign systems. This last proposal would be likely to be profitable only if future semiological investigations in other areas bore fruit. But Saussure's reason for making it seems to be primarily methodological, namely that whilst comparisons with legal and political institutions are likely to distract one from the essential features of language, comparisons with other human sign systems are less likely to do so. And since Saussure signally fails to make any such comparisons, the point is anyway arguably not materially important for the actual development of the argument of *CLG* (7.4).

If this is right, then the appeal to semiology amounts to little more than an outline of work that needs to be done. In particular, the characterisation of the nature of language developed so far is incomplete and cannot be completed until an account has been given of the nature of linguistic signs and of the way in which they form a system.

This account will form the subject matter of the next two chapters, but before we turn to them we must do three things: first, say something about Saussure's conception of a language as a form; second, discuss the relation of speech and writing to *langue* in Saussure's system; and finally, ask, once more, why he did not take the faculty of language as the object of enquiry.

2.2. Language as a form

Earlier we saw that Saussure maintains that sounds are only the instruments used by speakers to communicate and are of no intrinsic interest as such, any more than is the instrument used to transmit Morse Code. That is why sounds form the subject matter of the auxiliary science phonology, which it should be stressed again is not to be identified with what a modern linguist designates by that term. What is of primary interest to the linguist, by contrast, are not physical entities at all, but psychological entities (acoustic images and concepts) and the relations that obtain between them and other entities of the same kind:

> It [*langue*] is a system based on the mental oppositions of auditory impressions, just as a tapestry is a work of art produced by the visual oppositions of threads of different colors; the important thing in analysis is the role of oppositions, not the process through which the colors were obtained. (*CLG*, 56, 33)

So we must make a sharp distinction between, on the one hand, the entities belonging to *langue*, acoustic images and concepts, and the relations between them, and on the other the entities used to communicate (sounds, graphemes, etc.).

This claim leads to another central thesis, namely that language is a form, not a substance: 'Linguistics then works in the borderline where the elements of sound and thought combine; *their combination produces a form, not a substance*' (*CLG*, 157, 113). By this I take Saussure to mean that the significant distinctions belonging to *langue* are not based on independently identifiable distinctions in another medium, such as sound, but are, on the contrary, ones which provide principles of classification for that medium. In other words, the form of a language is a set of abstract relationships which are realisable in a particular medium or substance but which are not determined by the nature of that medium (Lyons 1968, 56).

Now, if language is a form and not a substance, it would seem that it is a matter of indifference which substance is utilised as its means of expression, provided that the abstract relationships are realisable in it. Various things Saussure himself says seem to commit him to such a view. For example, commenting on Whitney's claim that it is only through luck that we use the vocal organs as a means of expression, he says that 'the choice was more or less imposed by nature. But on the essential point the American linguist is right: language is a convention, and the nature of the sign that is agreed upon does not matter' (*CLG*, 26, 10). And a little later he argues that 'what is natural to mankind is not oral speech, but the faculty of constructing a language, i.e. a system of distinct signs corresponding to distinct ideas' (ibid.). So it seems to follow that not only is it a matter of indifference which substance is used, but there is no reason why one and the same language should not use different means of expression for different purposes, e.g., sounds for face-to-face communication and graphemes for writing, without either of them having a privileged position.

It is, therefore, surprising to find that this is a conclusion which Saussure rejects; though sounds are only the instrument of *langue*, they are nevertheless an instrument which has a special relation with it: 'Language and writing are two distinct systems of signs; the second exists for the sole purpose of representing the first. The linguistic object is not both the written and spoken forms of words; the spoken forms alone constitute the object' (*CLG*, 45, 23). This is to appeal to the first of the two analogies considered earlier, namely the analogy with a symphony, which is written for specific instruments, so that transcriptions are clearly derivative. The other analogy, with Morse Code, which

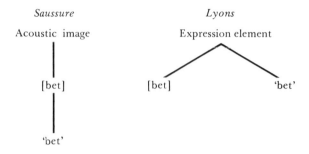

Figure 2.4

makes the question of the nature of the instrument a subordinate one, is at this point pushed into the background. But apart from the fact that relegating writing to the status of a secondary parasitic system seems to contradict the claim that it is a matter of indifference which kind of sign is agreed on, Saussure, when he writes that the spoken form alone constitutes the object, also seems to contradict his claim that acoustic images and concepts, and the relations between them, are the primary objects of interest to linguistics.

One diagnosis of what has gone wrong locates the problem with the term 'acoustic image'. This suggests that the entities that constitute *langue* are direct representations of sounds, but it is not clear why they have to be. If they were conceived of in a more abstract way, and called 'expression elements', following Lyons, then it would be possible to relate them both to representations of sounds indirectly by means of something analogous to morpho-phonemic rules and to representations of written words by a different set of rules. This would seem to be fully in the spirit of the idea that language is a form, and is the position adopted by Lyons in his admirably clear exposition of a version of structural linguistics which draws its inspiration from Saussure (1968, 60).[14] So a particular English word which is realised (indirectly) as a sequence of sounds by [bet], will be realised orthographically as 'bet'. Saussure's view is contrasted with Lyons's in Figure 2.4. It is clear, however, that such a solution would not have been acceptable to Saussure. For on this account it is difficult to see in what way the orthographic representation is parasitic on the phonological one, and is in fact a representation of it. For granting that historically speech always antedated writing, and that 'all systems of writing are demonstrably based upon units of spoken language' (Lyons 1968, 39), it does not follow that a written word actually represents its spoken form. And even Saussure would have to concede – particularly as this is part of his complaint about the tyranny of written language – that, once established, the written language would acquire a life of its own. Even if it started out as a parasitic system, it would become increasingly autonomous.

2.2.1. Derrida, Saussure, and writing

Pointing out these tensions and inconsistencies in Saussure's thought, Derrida has argued that they arise in part because Saussure for metaphysical reasons had to privilege sound:

> Although he recognised the necessity of putting the phonic substance between brackets ('What is essential in language, we shall see, is foreign to the phonic character of the linguistic sign' [p. 21]. 'In its essence it [the linguistic signifier] is not at all phonic' [p. 164]), Saussure for essential, and essentially metaphysical, reasons had to privilege speech, everything that links the sign to *phonē*. He also speaks of the 'natural link' between thought and voice, meaning and sound (p. 46). He even speaks of the 'thought-sound' (p. 156). (Derrida 1981, 21)

One reason Saussure had to privilege speech is that the very concept of a sign, which he employed because he could think of no other,

> carries within itself the necessity of privileging the phonic substance and of setting up linguistics as the 'pattern' for semiology. *Phonē*, in effect, is the signifying substance *given to consciousness* as that which is most intimately tied to the thought of the signified concept. From this point of view, the voice is consciousness itself. When I speak, not only am I conscious of being present for what I think, but I am conscious also of keeping as close as possible to my thought, or to the 'concept', a signifier that does not fall into the world, a signifier that I hear as soon as I emit it, that seems to depend upon my pure and free spontaneity, requiring the use of no instrument, no accessory, no force taken from the world. (Ibid.)

But granted for the moment that Saussure did subscribe to a metaphysics of presence, so that for him the meaning of a speaker's words is an expression of the speaker's thought, it is not obvious that in a manuscript culture speech sounds are for everyone the paradigm of a signifying substance. And it is even less obvious that the concept of a sign carries with it the necessity of privileging phonic substance; it is hard to see how for instance the sign language of the deaf does that (7.4). So though Derrida may be right that Saussure considered speech sounds to be the paradigm of a signifying substance, he certainly did not think that it was inevitable in a manuscript culture that everyone would be of the same opinion, for 'the spoken word is so intimately bound to its written image that the latter manages to usurp the main role. People attach even more importance to the written image of a vocal sign than to the sign itself' (*CLG*, 45, 24). In other words, it is not clear that Saussure thought that it was necessary from a phenomenological point of view to consider speech sounds as the paradigm case of a signifying substance.

Of course Derrida is right to draw attention to the fairly obvious tensions in Saussure's thought, in particular that between the view that, on the one hand, speech sounds are but one of many possible instruments which can be used to realise a language – the instruments as such being of no interest – and, on the other hand, the view that there is a particularly important connection between sounds and meaning. This difference is, of course, reflected in the difference between the Morse Code and symphonic models of the relationship between language and its instruments. Moreover, he is surely right to argue that Saussure's desubstantialised concept of the sign as a union of a 'concept' and an acoustic image is a not very promising starting point for a general semiology, if for no other reason than that 'it is difficult to see how it could be extended to every sign, be it phonetic-linguistic or not' (Derrida 1981, 22). For instance, as Derrida points out, 'theoretical mathematics . . . has never been absolutely linked with a phonetic production'; and

> beyond theoretical mathematics, the development of the *practical methods* of information retrieval extends the possibility of the 'message' vastly, to the point where it is no longer the 'written' translation of a language, the transporting of a signifier which could remain spoken in its integrity. (1976, 10)

2.2.2. *Writing and the recovery of the past*

A quite different reason why Saussure may have wished to privilege spoken language is suggested by Harris. It is concerned
with his desire to salvage something from the wreck of historical
linguistics. That he did wish to do this seems clear, for in contrast
to his treatment of phonology, the study of the speech sounds
utilised by a language, which he regards as an auxiliary discipline
belonging to *parole*, he treats phonetics, the study of the evolution
of sounds, as a 'basic part of the science of language' (*CLG*, 56,
33). But if it is, an acute problem arises about the evidential basis
of such a science. Clearly, much of our evidence exists only in
the form of written texts; but if writing is simply a different way
of expressing a language, then the written form will not be a
reliable guide to the spoken word. So, as Harris says, unless
writing has the status of a secondary parasitic system, which
represents *langue*,

> he would be obliged to conclude that in the case of dead languages
> a study of *la langue* ('the social product stored in the brain' [p.
> 44]) is impossible in principle. In other words most of the work
> done by Indo-Europeanists of Saussure's own generation would
> have to be excluded from linguistics. (1987, 43)

To which one might add: so would the work which made Saussure's own reputation.

This interpretation is certainly confirmed by the reasons Saussure gives for including a section on writing in a disquisition on
general linguistics. This is necessary because the linguist ought
to acquaint himself with the widest possible variety of languages.
However, 'we generally learn about languages only through writing' (*CLG*, 44, 23), and that is why it is necessary to consider
both its utility and its defects.

Moreover, this interpretation explains why Saussure was interested in an ideal alphabetic form of writing which would make
possible a completely faithful representation of the acoustic image (Harris 1987, 44).[15] It also explains why Saussure thought
that the fact that we can assimilate the system underlying dead
languages does not constitute a serious counterexample to the
primacy he allots to speech sounds. For if a writing system is
parasitic on a phonic system and is a more or less accurate rep-

resentation of it, then we cannot reconstruct the underlying *langue* without reconstructing the system of speech sounds it utilises. So, though as a reconstruction of what motivated Saussure this explanation has a more limited scope than Derrida's, it seems to me to be the more plausible explanation, given that Saussure did not wish to write off historical linguistics but rather to argue for a sharp separation of synchronic and diachronic issues.

That said, the existence of ideographic systems threatens to undermine Saussure's position entirely. In these cases, Saussure claims, the sign represents the whole word without representing its internal structure, the classic example of such a system being Chinese. However, since the ideogram may have a structure of its own which depends on quite different principles, there seems to be no warrant for saying that the ideogram represents the spoken word rather than that it is a different way of representing the same idea. The mere fact that there is a one-to-one correlation between spoken and written forms does not entitle us to say that the latter represent the former; there is such a correlation in Lyons's model, for instance. Oddly enough, Saussure admits as much: 'To a Chinese, an ideogram and a spoken word are both symbols of an idea; to him writing is a second language, and if two words that have the same sound are used in conversation, he may resort to writing in order to express his thought' (*CLG*, 48, 26). But this concession seems to be fatal to his overall position.

2.3. The faculty of language

Saussure's claim that 'what is natural to mankind is not oral speech, but the faculty of constructing a language' (*CLG*, 26, 10) and that 'beyond the functioning of the various organs there exists a more general faculty which governs signs and which would be the linguistic faculty proper' (*CLG*, 27, 11) prompted the question why the faculty in question should not be the object of enquiry (2.1.1). However, discussion of this question was postponed after notation of the germ of a possible answer to it, namely that the faculty cannot be exercised without the use of a *langue*, which is a social product.

But granting for the purpose of the argument that *langue* is indeed a cultural product, the fact that it is would be a reason for neglecting the faculty of language completely only if it were *wholly* a cultural product; that is, if the faculty made no contribution at all to the structure and content of *langue*. Now, it is arguable that Saussure does take care to ensure that the faculty makes no such contribution, for, as we saw, in his account of the way in which *langue* is assimilated he claims that the subject is passive.

However, that claim fails for at least three reasons. First, as I argued earlier, even if in a normal conversational situation the hearer's role is a purely passive one, that is irrelevant to the question of what is the role of a hearer learning a language from scratch. Second, in any case, the claim that the hearer's role in the normal speech situation is a passive one is not sustainable. For, apart from the fact that the hearer may have to resolve ellipsis, the words uttered may be ambiguous in a variety of ways. Consider

(4) I will take the old men and boys to the bank.

Interpretation of this will involve resolution of a grammatical ambiguity, 'old men and boys', and of a semantic one, 'bank', and a decision as to whether the utterance is a prediction or an undertaking. Third, nothing is said to rule out the possibility that the faculty of language does indeed play a role in the acquisition of language, though one of which the subject is unaware. Saussure could hardly object to this possibility on grounds of principle, since he allows that speakers internalise a representation of their *langue* without knowing that they do. So it is difficult to see how Saussure could exclude the possibility that the faculty of language makes a contribution, indeed possibly a large one, to the structure and content of *langue*.

It might be suggested that he is unworried by this possibility, because for him there is no such faculty, simply a more general sign faculty which is implicated in the use of any sign system (Harris 1987, 19). Linguistics then would not be concerned with such a faculty, since language is only one sign system and the study of it is not concerned with the other system, including writing. But, apart from the fact that to posit such a faculty would have been to draw a very large cheque on the yet to be developed discipline of semiology, surely questions analogous to those we asked about the faculty of language could be asked

about an all-purpose sign faculty. After all, Saussure believed
that there are semiological laws, so there is nothing strange for
him in the idea that a particular semiological system is constrained in various respects.

2.4. How abstract is *langue*?

Culler points out that the contrasts to which Saussure appeals
to distinguish *langue* from *parole* do not all draw the distinction
in the same place:

> ...in separating *langue* from *parole* one separates the essential
> from the contingent, the social from the purely individual, and
> the psychological from the material.... By the first [criterion] *la
> langue* is a wholly abstract and formal system; everything relating
> to sound is relegated to *parole* since English would still be essen-
> tially the same language if its units were expressed in some other
> way. But clearly, by the second criterion we would have to revise
> this view; the fact that /b/ is a voiced bilabial stop and /p/ a voiceless
> bilabial stop is a fact about the linguistic system in that the indi-
> vidual speaker cannot choose to realize the phonemes differently
> if he is to continue speaking English. And by the third criterion
> one would have to admit other acoustic differences to *la langue*,
> since differences between accent and pronunciations have a psy-
> chological reality for speakers of a language. (1976, 81)

These points are well taken; evidence of Saussure's own uncertainty is the fact that he sometimes likens *langue* to Morse Code,
an abstract system implementable in many different ways, and
to an orchestra score, which is meant to be implemented in a
very specific way.

The difference between these metaphors corresponds to the
distinction between a *schema* and a *norm* drawn by Hjelmslev,
who argued that the simple dichotomy between *langue* and *parole*
drawn by Saussure should be replaced by a more complicated
set of distinctions among *schema*, *norms*, *usage*, and *parole*.

> Usage is a statistical regularity: one can chart the frequency of
> different pronunciations or of other uses of linguistic elements.
> A speaker of a language has a certain freedom in his choice of
> usage. The norm, however is not a matter of individual choice.
> It is not described statistically but represented as a series of rules:

e.g. the phoneme /p/ is realized in English as a voiceless bilabial stop. Finally the schema is the most abstract conception of structure. Here there is no reference to phonic substance. Elements are defined in abstract relational terms: /p/ is to /b/ as /t/ is to /d/, and it is irrelevant what actual features are used to manifest these differences. (Ibid.)

Clearly we get very different conceptions of *langue* depending on whether we identify it with a schema, a schema plus a set of norms, or a schema and both a set of norms and a set of usages. The Morse Code analogy articulates the first of these conceptions, whilst that of the orchestra articulates the second. But which is Saussure's real view? It is tempting to argue that he does not really have to choose, since these views simply represent descriptions of the same thing at different levels of abstraction. But, as we shall see, an assumption Saussure makes later when developing the theory of the sign, that it is a two-sided entity, makes it difficult if not impossible for him to adopt this view (3.1, 7.1). As it is, he vacillates between the conception of *langue* as schema and as norm.

2.5. Summary and prospect

We have seen that to make his central distinction between *langue* and *parole* Saussure has to distinguish three terms, natural language – *langage*; a particular language – *langue*; and speech – *parole*. Moreover, though his arguments against treating speech sounds as the subject matter of linguistics are convincing, as is his contention that language (*langage*) has both social and individual aspects, the nature of the central dichotomy remains unclear in a variety of respects. One problem stems from the nature of the definition employed, which involves division of a field of enquiry the extent of which is assumed to be antecedently clear. But, as we saw, this is just not so. It is unclear precisely what totality of linguistic facts is meant to be included in *langage*, given the inherent vagueness of the term 'linguistic fact'. So it is hardly surprising that, whatever one takes *langue* to be, the 'remainder', *parole,* should turn out to comprise a heterogeneous collection of very diverse kinds of things. But surely no conclusion of substance can follow from this; for instance, that *parole* does not merit serious study. The proper conclusion is that it comprises a variety of areas which may well merit serious study, and that talk of a dichotomy is dangerously misleading if it blinds us to that fact.

I have argued that Saussure's claim that *langue* is the object of linguistics should not be undertood to entail that it and only it should be studied. What is claimed is not this, but rather that reconstruction of a *langue* is an essential prerequisite to any kind of serious linguistic enquiry. This interpretation makes Saussure's interest in historical and geographical linguistics intelligible, which the first does not. As for Saussure's claim that *langue* is social, that would seem not to involve any commitment to a supra-individual mind, so it does not involve any dubious reification of that sort. The only mental states there are are those of individuals. What makes *langue* social is the explanation of how members of the same linguistic community acquire similar representations, i.e., how they come to associate systematically the same concept with the same acoustic-image, and the role those representations play in face-to-face communication. This is, no doubt, somewhat cryptic as it stands; we shall return to a more detailed discussion of this issue in Chapter 7.

Since, as I have argued, the characterisation of *langue* is incomplete, because the way in which it constitutes a system has yet to be explained, an evaluation of the utility of Saussure's concept is not appropriate at this point. Nevertheless, there are a number of questions about the way in which the concept was introduced. In the first place, we are never told why the speech-circuit model is the appropriate model to appeal to; yet there seem to be a number of important assumptions implicit in that appeal. Second, Saussure's arguments showing that *langue* is passive, that is that individuals have no active role to play in its acquisition, seem to be quite inadequate to demonstrate that this is so. As a result, his attempt to exclude a role for the faculty of language in language acquisition, which would, if it existed, diminish the importance of social factors, is a failure. Third, it is not easy to see what is to be gained by treating *langue* as a semiological system in the absence of any account of what such a system contains.

Perhaps the best answer Saussure could give to this last comment is to demonstrate the value of adopting the semiological approach in his explanation of the way in which *langue* constitutes a system. That, anyway, is what he seems to do; and it is to that explanation that we now turn.

3

LANGUAGE AS A SYSTEM
OF SIGNS
I: Signs, arbitrariness, linearity, and change

The title 'Language as a System of Signs' was proposed by Saussure himself for Part 1, Chapter 1, of *CLG*, but for some reason the editors ignored his suggestion. I have used it as part of my title because it encapsulates a central point in Saussure's theory, namely that a language (*langue*) is a system of signs forming a well-defined object which can be studied independently of the other aspects of natural language. Thus, as was argued in the preceding chapter, the ideas in this and later chapters of *CLG* can be seen as deepening the characterisation of *langue* developed so far. As we shall see, there are many occasions on which Saussure returns to points raised earlier.

Clearly, there are two central ideas to be introduced now, that of a sign and that of a system. To develop the former, Saussure introduces two key principles, the Arbitrary Nature of the Sign and the Linear Nature of the Signifier. The first of these has been the object of a great deal of discussion; the second has occasioned much less comment despite Saussure's claim that it is as important. As we shall see, each principle has a major role to play in Saussure's overall argument. However, the characterisation of them in Part 1, Chapter 1, is only partial, and Saussure expands it in a number of important ways in later chapters. For instance, his discussion in Part 1, Chapter 2, of the question why,

47

if a sign is arbitrary, an individual – indeed, a community – is nevertheless not free to change it is an important development of the idea of arbitrariness. Moreover, this discussion of the reasons why languages are both resistant and vulnerable to change introduces for the first time temporal considerations into Saussure's account, thus raising a number of important issues which call for further discussion.

My next chapter, Chapter 4, will describe how consideration of the effect of time on language leads Saussure to formulate the second major dichotomy of *CLG*, that between synchronic and diachronic approaches to language, and to give a preliminary outline of the precise way in which a language constitutes a very special kind of system, 'a system of pure values which are determined by nothing except the momentary arrangements of its terms' (*CLG*, 116, 80). Saussure's detailed description of this system will be reserved for Chapter 5; whilst Chapter 6 will complete the outline of his main argument by considering his account of linguistic value and its dependence on a system.

3.1. Language is not a nomenclature

As we saw in 1.2, Saussure was opposed to nomenclaturism, the view that language 'is a naming-process only – a list of words, each corresponding to the thing that it names' (*CLG*, 97, 65). The only element of truth in this picture, Saussure claims, is the conception of a linguistic unit as a 'double entity' the two parts of which are joined by association. But otherwise the view is seriously mistaken: It assumes the existence of ideas that antedate words; it leaves it unclear whether a word is a vocal or a psychological entity; and it assumes far too simple a picture of the relation between a name and what it names.

However, as Harris points out, it is by no means clear that all versions of nomenclaturism are subject to Saussure's objection. So the best way to proceed at this point is not to try to evaluate his attack in general terms, but to see what particular version of nomenclaturism Saussure objected to, and how compelling are his objections to it.[1]

The extensive manuscript note used by the editors to supplement the students' notes at this point makes it clear that the main target was comparative linguistics (Engler 2, 148F). Treating a word as a double entity, e.g., as a signifier correlated with something else, might suggest that it is possible to trace the history of a word of which the meaning remains fixed but which is expressed in different ways in different languages. From this point of view, there is nothing wrong in principle with the suggestion that the Latin word *arbor* and the French word *arbre* express the same idea using different means, since the idea expressed is not tied to any particular form of expression. But, as we saw (1.2.), Saussure believed that this was a mistake; the changes in time that affect the form of expression also affect the idea expressed. For instance, the Latin *crimen* (accusation) became our 'crime'.

In sharp contrast to the comparativists, Saussure held that there are no language-independent meanings.[2] It is true, of course, that the kind of argument adduced which appeals to changes of the *crimen*/'crime' sort is purely empirical. So even though Saussure cites many instances of changes of form that are also changes of meaning, what is badly needed at this point is a theoretical justification of his position. There is no doubt that it is his position.

Moreover, Saussure's stance on the other two issues raised – viz., how complex is the relation between a name and what it names, and whether signs are vocal or psychological – is closely connected to his claim that there are no language-independent meanings. For if there are none, then it is plausible to suppose that the meaning which a particular item has depends in some way on its intralinguistic relations to other items in the language rather than on its relation to something extralinguistic, so that if it is a name of something it is so only because of the role it plays in the language as a whole. And if it is knowledge of a sign's intralinguistic relations which enables members of a linguistic community to engage in communication, then those relations must be psychologically real. This is an assumption which is obviously central to Saussure's speech-circuit model, which in effect treats the relations as holding between psychological entities, which, though they are not called such in his exposition, are signs. Hence, for him a word is a psychological entity.[3]

So the position that Saussure tries to establish is that a linguistic sign is a psychological entity related systematically to other linguistic signs to form a system, and furthermore one whose signifying features depend on the ways in which it is related to those other signs. But before trying to trace his argument, it is

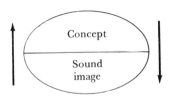

Figure 3.1

worth stressing that he does retain a relic of nomenclaturism in
the assumption that a sign is a 'double entity' in a surprisingly
uncritical way, and that one of the more difficult things he has
to do is to explain why, if each sign has a double aspect, neither
of the aspects can exist independently of the other.

3.1.1. Linguistic signs

In one fairly natural usage, if a word expresses an idea it might
be said that it is a sign of an idea. But this usage is not Saussure's.
For him, a sign does involve two things, an acoustic image and
a concept, but he does not think of the former as a sign of the
latter. On the contrary, the sign is the union of both of them,
and can be represented as in Figure 3.1. We are by now familiar
with the term 'acoustic image' which is explained here as the
'psychological imprint of the sound, the impression that it makes
on our senses' (*CLG*, 98, 66). This explanation troubled the editors, who worried whether it should not also include a representation of the movements involved in articulation, presumably
to account for its role in execution as well as that in reception
(ibid.). But the point is that though Saussure's term 'acoustic
image' makes it very natural to think of it as an image, there
would seem to be no need to do so. The *psychological* imprint
could be quite abstract given the role it plays in the speech-circuit
model; all that is necessary is that there should be systematic
correlations between it and speech sounds, whether uttered or
heard.

   In an earlier discussion we saw that the editors retained the
pair of terms 'acoustic image'/'concept' for the original explanation of a sign, ignoring Saussure's instruction to use the pair
'signifier'/'signified' instead (1.3). They do introduce the latter
pair later:

I propose to retain the word *sign* [*signe*] to designate the whole and to replace *concept* and *sound-image* respectively by *signified* [*signifié*] and *signifier* [*signifiant*]; the last two terms have the advantage of indicating the opposition that separated them from each other and from the whole of which they are parts. (*CLG*, 99, 67)

But the only reason they give for coining the new terms is as a corrective to the tendency to think of the acoustic image itself, e.g., *arbor*, as the sign, rather than the union of it with a concept. Inevitably, the reader is left with the impression that 'signified' is a near-synonym for 'concept' and merely has different associations, whereas, as we shall see, Saussure tries to elucidate the notion of a signified in terms of the notion of a value, albeit a very special kind of value arising from social usage (6.1). So the suggested identification of a signified with a concept, and not even a concept of a special kind, is, to say the least, unfortunate, since the dangers of lapsing into the sort of nomenclaturist theory that Saussure so objected to are clear.[4]

Arguably, the editors had no option but to retain the term 'acoustic image', since one of Saussure's central theses is that a signifier is an acoustic image, though the 'is' in question is presumably not one of identity, since there are acoustic images which are not signifiers. However, it might be argued that analogously they were right to retain the term 'concept', since a signified is a concept, albeit one of a special kind.

Certainly for the speech-circuit model to play any part in Saussure's argument, a signified has to be able to fulfil the role allocated to a concept in that model. So perhaps what we are witnessing at this point is an attempt to reconcile two apparently contrary tendencies in Saussure's thought, the psychologism implicit in the speech-circuit model on the one hand, and the emphasis on the social character of language which leads him to treat a signified as a special kind of value on the other. Perhaps that tension is resolvable, but until it is resolved the mixture of terminologies is undoubtedly confusing. To avoid such confusion we should, at this stage, think of the new terms 'signifier'/ 'signified' as theoretical terms whose content has to be explained by reference to the role they play in a theory that has yet to be developed, rather than as near-synonyms of the old pair 'acoustic image'/'concept'.

Now, according to Saussure, linguistic signs have two 'primordial characteristics'. They are arbitrary, and their signifiers are linear. It is to these two key theses that we now turn.

3.2. Linguistic signs are arbitrary

This is so, Saussure argues, because the bond between the signifier and the signified is arbitrary, a point which he illustrates as follows:

> The idea of 'sister' is not linked by any inner relationship to the succession of sounds s-ö-r which serves as its signifier in French; that it could be represented equally by just any other sequence is proved by differences among languages and by the very existence of different languages: the signified 'ox' has as its signifier b-ö-f on one side of the border and o-k-s (Ochs) on the other. (CLG, 100, 67)

But though this explanation of what he meant is clear, it has seemed to many not to be clearly to Saussure's purpose, since it apparently rests on the very kind of nomenclaturist assumption that he objected to so strongly, and so provides an illustration of the danger of retaining the conception of the sign as a two-sided entity. Hence Jakobson's comment that

> this theory is in blatant contradiction with the most valuable and the most fertile ideas of Saussurian linguistics. This theory would have us believe that different languages use a variety of signifiers to correspond to one common and unvarying signified, but it was Saussure himself who, in his Course, correctly defended the view that the meanings of words themselves vary from one language to another. The scope of the word boeuf and that of the word Ochs do not coincide. (1978, 111)

Now, the assumption which is made by the example about the differing signifiers of 'ox', that one and the same idea can be expressed in different languages by different means, is just the sort of nomenclaturist assumption that Saussure objected to, so Jakobson's point is well taken.[5] But does Jakobson also wish to maintain that the connection, which is a purely intralinguistic one, between b-ö-f and its signified 'boeuf' is not arbitrary? Apparently he does, for he quotes with approval Benveniste's claim

that 'the connection between the signifier and the signified is not
arbitrary; on the contrary it is necessary' (1966, 50). This is so
because 'the two have been imprinted on my mind together;
they are mutually evocative in all circumstances. There is between them such an intimate symbiosis that the concept "boeuf"
is like the soul of the acoustic image *b-ö-f*' (ibid., 51). It is, however, difficult to believe that Saussure would have denied this,
for later, expanding on the sense in which the sign is arbitrary,
he says:

> The term should not be taken to imply that the choice is left
> entirely to the speaker (we shall see below that the individual does
> not have the power to change a sign in any way once it has become
> established in the linguistic community); I mean that it is un-
> motivated, i.e. arbitrary in that it actually has no natural connec-
> tion with the signified. (*CLG*, 101, 68)

In other words, Saussure would agree with Benveniste that the
connection is indeed one which has been imprinted on the minds
of French-speakers, and one moreover which no individual can
change. Nevertheless, he wants to say that it is arbitrary.

Part of what he means is that another sequence of sounds,
e.g., *s-ö-f*, might have become the signifier of 'boeuf'. This is not
to say that as things are adult French-speakers could change
their speech habits, but it is to claim that if *s-ö-f* had been the
signifier of 'boeuf' when they learned French they would have
learned to use it as such, so that they would produce the sequence
s-ö-f whenever they now produce the sequence *b-ö-f*.[6] As Lévi-
Strauss says, the sign is arbitrary *a priori*, but non-arbitrary *a
posteriori*. That is, there is no intrinsic connection between *b-ö-f*
and 'boeuf' but once the former becomes the signifier of the
latter in French, a French-speaker has no option but to relate
them in that way.

It must indeed be conceded that Saussure's explanation of
what he means by 'arbitrary' is fairly casual, though it should be
remembered that it was his practice to introduce key distinctions
quite sketchily before going on to develop them in detail; this
case is no exception. However, more must be said at this point
about the term 'unmotivated', used to explain his notion of
arbitrariness.

Clearly, a claim to the effect that the relation between a signifier and its signified is unmotivated, that is that they are not naturally connected, excludes many different possibilities. It would be difficult to enumerate them, but in general terms, in all of these cases some fact about the world makes the signifier an appropriate one for its signified.

For instance, it might be argued that the fact that cuckoos produce a certain sort of sound makes the English word 'cuckoo' an appropriate one for its signified. The word 'cuckoo' is, of course, onomatopoeic; that is, there is a similarity between the sound produced when it is pronounced and the characteristic call of the bird it denotes. In Saussurean terminology, it is the similarity of the signifier of the sign to the sound produced by cuckoos which makes the signifier an appropriate one for its signified. In other words, what makes the signifier appropriate are facts about cuckoos and sounds and signifiers.

Onomatopoeia is one of the two *prima facie* counterexamples to the principle of the Arbitrariness of the Sign discussed by Saussure. The other involves interjections, in which one is tempted to see, he says, 'spontaneous expressions of reality dictated, so to speak, by natural forces' (*CLG*, 101, 69). For instance, if when hurt I naturally make the sound [ouch], then the word 'ouch' is appropriate for the expression of that feeling because of the similarity of the sound produced when it is pronounced to the natural expression.

Saussure's treatment of these counterexamples is reminiscent of Hume's treatment of a counterexample to the principle that all ideas come from antecedent impressions, viz., that it exists but is of small account in relation to the overall principle. Thus Saussure argues that genuine onomatopoeic signs are rare; that they are only approximate imitations of natural sounds; and that they become subject to morphological and phonological evolution. His discussion of interjections is even briefer; but there seems to be no reason to quarrel with the overall conclusion that 'onomatopoeic formations and interjections are of secondary importance, and their symbolic origin is in part open to dispute' (*CLG*, 102, 70).[7]

But what is surprising is that though it is clear that the number of possible varieties of motivation that have to be excluded is very great indeed, no attempt is made to enumerate them and to consider them carefully. The reader is simply left with the impression that the counterexamples are of little account. In-

deed, we are left thinking that all that is at issue is the question
of whether there are non-linguistic facts which make certain
signifiers appropriate for their signifieds, as in onomatopoeia;
but in fact there are many other possible kinds of motivation
which Saussure wishes to exclude.

This can easily be seen by noting that Port Royal grammarians
(1.2) could readily agree about the marginality of onomatopoeia
and interjections, and continue to maintain that linguistic categories correspond to conceptual categories – noun phrases to
substances, adjectives to modes, etc. – and that the structure of
sentences corresponds to that of thoughts.[8] In other words, they
could maintain that the categories of our grammar and the structures of our sentences are motivated by the categories of logic
and the structures of our thoughts. So we need to distinguish at
least three levels of motivation: that of signifiers, as in onomatopoeia; categorial motivation, by which we mean the determination, partial at least, by non-linguistic facts of the lexical,
syntactical, or morphological etc. categories of a language; and
structural motivation, that is the determination, at least partial,
by non-linguistic facts of the structure of phrases and sentences.

A strong version of the autonomy of language must exclude
all three kinds of motivation. But evidently if Saussure does wish
to do this, then the arguments adduced to date go a very small
way indeed towards establishing his overall conclusion. However,
as I said, it is Saussure's custom to explain new distinctions only
partially when introducing them and then to deepen the explanations later (*TM*, 443). So, for the moment, the only possible
verdict about the thesis that signs are unmotivated is that Saussure has gone only a little way to show that this is so.

3.2.1. The scope of the principle

Before I close this discussion something must be said about the
scope of Saussure's principle of arbitrariness. Does it apply to
all linguistic signs, however complex, or only to some?

In the section under discussion Saussure gives no guidance,
so the reader is entitled to conclude that, for instance, 'twenty-
seven' is as arbitrary as are its component signs 'twenty' and
'seven'. However, Saussure argues later that we should distinguish between the complex sign and the simple signs of which
it is composed. Only the latter are completely arbitrary; the for-

mer is constructed in accordance with a pattern, 'twenty-one, twenty-two, ..., thirty-one, thirty-two, ...', and for this reason is said by Saussure to be only relatively unmotivated: 'Some signs are absolutely arbitrary; in other words we note, not its complete absence, but the presence of degrees of arbitrariness: *the sign may be relatively motivated*' (*CLG*, 180, 131). This suggests that the principle of the Arbitrariness of the Sign has universal scope but that only those signs which are not modelled on productive patterns internal to the language are completely arbitrary, the remainder being relatively arbitrary.

However, the notion of relative arbitrariness muddies the waters. The feature of 'twenty-one' that Saussure describes as relative arbitrariness is not a less absolute form of arbitrariness than that exhibited by 'twenty' and 'one' – after all, there is nothing more natural about 'twenty-one' than there is about 'one and twenty' – but an example of something quite different: linguistic system. In other words, the concept of relative arbitrariness rests on a confusion between the idea of motivation and that of linguistic system (5.2.1). This is so because the root idea of motivation is that of the determination of a linguistic feature by something extralinguistic, whilst that of linguistic system is that of intralinguistic determination.[9] It may well be that it is *because* the sign is arbitrary that linguistic system is important, as Saussure argues: 'Everything that relates to language as a system must, I am convinced, be approached from this viewpoint, which has scarcely received the attention of linguists: the limiting of arbitrariness' (*CLG*, 182, 133). But to call a system a species of arbitrariness, relative arbitrariness, not only is confusing but distracts attention away from the important question. What features, if any, must such a system have?

3.3. The signifier is linear

The first principle was about signs, but the second is a thesis only about signifiers. As I said, it has occasioned much less discussion. Moreover, when it has been discussed it has provoked puzzlement, on the grounds that it is clear neither what it means nor what its role in Saussure's system is.[10] Nevertheless, Saussure thought it as important as the first principle, since 'the whole mechanism of language depends upon it' (*CLG*, 103, 70). By this he seems to mean that without this principle his account of the way in which a language is constituted by a system of relations of a special kind, that is syntagmatic and associative ones, would fall to the ground (5.3).

Now, it is important to remember at this point that Saussure's principle concerns only signifiers, and that signifiers are acoustic images. As such they are representations of speech sounds but are not themselves speech sounds; just as maps may represent a hilly terrain, which has three dimensions, without themselves being three-dimensional, so can an acoustic image represent things which have properties it does not.

This is important, because it is easy to suppose that Saussure is claiming that signifiers themselves are linear, and then to object that there is no need for them to be so even if what they represent is linear, which is correct (Henry 1970, 89). It would therefore be nice if one could report that Saussure does not confuse properties of the signifier with properties of what it represents. Unfortunately, it is not completely clear that he is not guilty of this confusion, for he writes: 'The signifier, being auditory, is unfolded solely in time from which it gets the following characteristics: (a) it represents a span, and (b) the span is measurable in a single dimension; it is a line' (*CLG*, 103, 70). Uncharitably, one could take him to be saying that signifiers partake of a property of what they represent; namely, they unfold in time.

However, it is not clear that this is what he means. For the question which concerns him seems to be: What are the constraints imposed on signifiers as representations by the fact that the medium in which they are realised is auditory? His answer is that because the medium represented is auditory, as representations signifiers have to represent a span of time, which has a linear character. This interpretation is borne out by what he says a little later. 'In contrast to visual signifiers (nautical signals, etc.) which can offer simultaneous groupings in several dimensions, auditory signifiers have at their command only the dimension of time. Their elements are represented in succession; they form a chain' (ibid.). His point here seems to be clear. Whereas a visual signal can utilise a number of different features at the same time (shape and colour, for instance), this is not true of an auditory signal; it can utilise only temporal features, so that it is only these features which an auditory signifier can represent. So, whether or not he failed to make a categorial distinction between signifiers and what they represent, the point he is making does not depend on confusing these very different things.

The point that the principle is one about signifiers is also important because it means that counterexamples appealing to the properties of elements that are not signifiers are, on the face of it, not relevant, so that arguments appealing to phonology are beside the point. These arguments turn on the fact that phonemes can be analysed into bundles of features; /m/ and /n/, for instance, have the same features except for the fact that the latter is nasal and the former is not. Thus Jakobson, in a severe criticism of Saussure, writes:

> Bally, faithful to his master's doctrine, arrived at the thesis that it is impossible to pronounce two sounds at the same time! This argument is a *petitio principii*. . . . Two phonemes cannot be emitted simultaneously. But it is perfectly possible to emit several distinctive features at the same time. Not only is this possible, it is what is normally done, since *phonemes are complex entities*. (1978, 99)

But if, as Jakobson himself points out, 'the phoneme . . . differs from all other linguistic values in that it is not endowed with any specific meaning' (ibid., 61) – its role being to differentiate items which do have meaning – then it is not a signifier (which does have a meaning, since it is associated with a signified). So the fact that a phoneme can be further analysed into a set of distinctive features is not a counterexample to Saussure's principle, which is a principle about signifiers (*TM*, 447).

This argument has been challenged by Harris. He points out that Saussure speaks of the *elements* of signifiers forming a chain, and adds that

> the putative counterexample to the principle of linearity which Saussure raises and rejects in the final paragraph is the phenomenon of syllabic stress. The example would scarcely make sense if linearity were only a principle which applied to the syntagmatic relationship between one *signifiant* and the next, but did not apply to the speech chain *in toto*. (1987, 71)

Harris's points are well taken. However, they are not conclusive. The expression 'their elements' could be taken to refer to phonemes amongst other things, but it is certainly not necessary to take it so, particularly since Saussure did not think that the sounds which realise signifiers literally constitute them. Instead, Saussure could have been referring to the elements of a complex signifier, e.g., 'twenty-one', whose elements would be simple signifiers. And, as far as I can see, the point about syllabic stress would constitute a putative counterexample only if the stressed syllable were a signifier, so that the stress modified what was signified in some way.

Whether this is right or not, the crucial question is what role the principle of linearity plays in Saussure's system. What he himself says is, as we saw, quite explicit, namely that the crucial account developed later of the relations which signifiers can enter into (5.3) depends on it, though unfortunately he does not say why he thinks this is so. A reasonable conjecture at this point would therefore be that the principle is meant to explain why signifiers can have these, and only these, relations. Certainly without such an explanation there is a serious lacuna in his overall position, since there is no theoretical justification for his claim that signifiers can enter into only the kinds of relations that he describes.

If I am right, his argument is that because the medium in which signifiers are realised is auditory, they can enter into only the kinds of relations he describes later. And whatever one thinks of such an argument, it is quite clear that an argument is needed at this point. This is especially clear if one assumes that Saussure has adopted a semiological approach, so that his aim is to derive a detailed description of the nature of a linguistic system from fundamental principles about signs (7.4).

But as well as a justificatory role, the principle has also a methodological role, as Harris points out (1987, 77). For when we are confronted with a complex signifier such as 'one hundred and seventy-one', all that the principle of the Arbitrariness of the Sign can tell us is that it is arbitrary, and that so are its constituent signifiers. But it alone cannot tell us how to segment it into constituent signifiers; to do this another principle is needed. So, Harris argues, if the premiss is accepted that spoken language is articulated as a concatenated succession of linked elements, then 'by combining both Saussurean principles linguistics is immediately provided with a method of analysis, which will consist basically of segmenting any given catenary sequence by determining which arbitrary sets of consecutive elements in the se-

quence could constitute single *signifiants* and which could not'
(ibid., 77). And indeed one account that Saussure gives of linguistic analysis does fit this description.[11]

However, if it is clear both what the role of the principle is,
and that such a principle is needed for the development of his
theory, it is very far from clear that the principle does the job
it is intended to do. For, to anticipate Saussure's account of the
'mechanisms' of language (5.3), only one of the relations he posits
has a linear character:

> In discourse, on the one hand, words acquire relations based on
> the linear nature of language because they are chained together.
> This rules out the possibility of pronouncing two elements si-
> multaneously.... The elements are arranged simultaneously on
> the chain of speaking. Combinations supported by linearity are
> *syntagms*. (*CLG*, 170, 123)

Examples he gives of syntagms range from complex words like
're-read' to sentences. But as well as syntagmatic relations, there
is another kind of important relation, which Saussure calls 'associative': 'Outside discourse, on the other hand, words acquire
relations of a different kind. Those that have something in common are associated in the memory, resulting in groups marked
by diverse relations' (*CLG*, 171, 123). For instance, 'painful'
might call to mind 'delightful', 'frightful', etc., so that a particular
word is 'at the point of convergence of an indefinite number of
co-ordinated terms'. And it is, as we shall see, a cardinal point
of Saussure's theory that our understanding of a particular signifier involves knowing not only what syntagmatic relations it
has, but also what associative relations it has.

At this point, Saussure's developed theory is an outright contradiction of the principle of Linearity, which says not merely
that the signifier represents a span – which in itself would not
lead to contradiction – but that the span is measureable in only
a single dimension. However, as Jakobson rightly says, the developed theory insists that two dimensions or axes are relevant:

> He rigorously distinguished two axes: '(1) *the axis of simultaneity*
> (AB) which concerns relations between coexisting things, and
> from which any intervention by time is excluded, and (2) the *axis
> of succession* (CD).

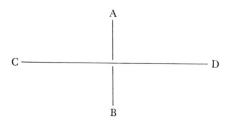

(1978, 100)

The only possible conclusion is therefore that, far from under-pinning the account that Saussure gives of the mechanisms of language, the principle of Linearity contradicts it, since it denies what the developed theory affirms, namely that signifiers are locatable in a two-dimensional conceptual space.

3.4. The sign is both immutable and mutable

The editors thought that Saussure's claim, made in Part 1, Chapter 2, that the sign is both mutable and immutable was sufficiently paradoxical to call for editorial explanation, namely that he wanted to stress that languages change in spite of the inability of speakers to change them (*CLG*, 108, 74). But his thesis was not quite as banal as that. He wanted to argue that the semiological factors which explain why languages are stable also explain why they change. In essence his explanation is that they are both resistant to and vulnerable to change because they are historically constituted social institutions which, being founded on the principle of the Arbitrariness of the Sign, have no rational basis. In this respect they are quite unlike all other institutions.

This discussion considers languages (*langues*) in relation to the historical factors, operating in time, that affect them. As it develops, characterisations of both the ways in which *langue* is social and the sign is arbitrary are extended considerably. It is also an important discussion because in introducing the topic of time it leads on to the introduction of the other central Saussurean dichotomy, that between synchronic and diachronic linguistics.

3.4.1. Why languages are stable

We saw earlier, when looking at Benveniste's objections to Saussure's principle of the Arbitrariness of the Sign (3.2), that Saussure asserts that neither the individual nor the community as a whole has the power to change a sign once it is established. But why is this so?

To begin with, Saussure argues, a language (*langue*) is never invented by its users; it is always inherited, the product of historical forces. However, since it hardly follows that what is inherited cannot be changed by collective agreement, we must ask 'why the historical factor of transmission dominates it entirely and prohibits any sudden widespread change' (*CLG*, 105, 72).

There are, Saussure claims, four main reasons why this is so. First, because the sign is arbitrary, there is no rational basis for a discussion about whether or not to change it: 'There is no reason for preferring *soeur* to *sister*, *Ochs* to *boeuf*, etc.' (*CLG*, 106, 73). Second, there are a multiplicity of signs. One can envisage the replacement of one writing system by another precisely because it contains some twenty to forty letters. By contrast, linguistic signs are numberless. The sheer size of the system makes it difficult to grasp, let alone change. Third, the fact that it is a system which can be understood only by specialists means that the masses cannot transform it, because they are unaware of it. Finally, language is a very special kind of institution. Most institutions involve only some people some of the time, but 'in language, on the contrary, everyone participates at all times' (*CLG*, 107, 73). So, because it is very difficult to get everyone to change a habit, particularly when there is no rational basis for change, language is like an inert mass that is highly resistant to individual initiative.

One further factor needs to be mentioned, Saussure argues, and that is time. Because language is inherited and signs are arbitrary, they rest on tradition. 'We say *man* and *dog* because our predecessors said *man* and *dog*' (*CLG*, 108, 74). So solidarity with our traditions and customs is another factor, in addition to the inertia of the collectivity, that makes for stability. One can see what he means. There is an evident disutility in attempts to depart radically from established social customs. By convention, one stops when traffic lights are red and moves again when they change to green. An alternative convention is imaginable, viz.

stopping when they are green and moving on red. But it would obviously be most unwise to adopt this as one's practice unless one was sure that everyone else would do the same. Analogously, if one wishes to be understood, to adopt perfectly conceivable alternatives to 'man' and 'dog' has no point unless one is sure that others will do the same.[12]

It is now clear why Saussure thinks that the fact that signs are arbitrary does not imply that either an individual, by stipulation, or a group, by collective agreement, can change a sign. Nevertheless, his arguments do not exclude change *tout court*; what they do, or are meant to do, is to exclude change that comes about by design. Though Saussure does not deny that there is scope for individual variation, what he does claim is that there are many factors which make it difficult for it to become established, i.e., to affect *langue*. Moreover, if it does, the resulting change is never one that was designed: 'In contrast to the false notion that we readily fashion for ourselves about it, a language is not a mechanism created and arranged with a view to the concepts to be expressed' (*CLG*, 121, 85). But if there is scope for individual variation, the combined weights of tradition and the social collectivity seem to be so powerful that one might wonder why a language subjugated to them both does not become completely static. In other words, the problem now is to explain how change is possible at all.

3.4.2. Why languages are mutable

One would expect Saussure, before answering this question, to review the kinds of change there can be in a language and the sorts of factors that might be responsible for them, just as he reviewed the sorts of factors responsible for stability. But in fact he does this in only the sketchiest of ways, if at all. After saying that changes can take many forms, he says:

> One might think that it [change] deals especially with phonetic changes undergone by the signifier, or perhaps changes in meaning which affect the signified concept. The view would be inadequate. Regardless of what the forces of change are, whether in isolation or in combination, they always result in *a shift in the relationship between the signified and signifier*. (*CLG*, 109, 75)

For instance, the Latin *necàre* (to kill) became *noyer* (to drown) in French. In this case, both signifier and signified have changed, but, Saussure seems to argue, one should not treat these as two independent phenomena: '...it is sufficient to state with respect to the whole that the bond between the idea and the sign was loosened, and that there was a shift in their relationship' (ibid.).

This looks very much like changing the subject from the topic of the admittedly very various factors responsible for change, to that of their effect, which is said to be always the same, namely a shift in the relation between signifier and signified. But why that is their only possible effect is never explained – though, as we shall see later, there are a number of theoretical reasons why Saussure has to say that signs cannot change (4.2). Clearly, it is far from obvious, given the principle of the Arbitrariness of the Sign, that every change in a signifier will result in a new relationship with its signified. The kind of change involved in using *s-ö-f* instead of *b-ö-f* as the signifier for 'boeuf' should, according to the principle, leave that relation unchanged. So what is the force of claiming that in such a case the relation of the new signifier to its signified is different from that of the old one to its?

Turning, then, to Saussure's explanation why, in spite of the weight of the collectivity and of tradition, change nevertheless occurs, it is perhaps unsurprising that he has not got a great deal to say, for he has at this stage said nothing at all about the factors responsible for change. His main point is: 'Language is radically powerless to defend itself against the forces which from one moment to the next are shifting the relationship between the signified and signifier. This is one of the consequences of the arbitrary nature of the sign' (*CLG*, 110, 75). The kinds of changes that can occur in other institutions are limited precisely because they are not completely arbitrary. Fashion, for instance, is constrained by the shape of the human body; but there is no analogous restraint in the case of human language. So one of the factors which make it difficult to change languages, their arbitrariness, at the same time renders them vulnerable to change.

At the risk of labouring the obvious, it should be said that this satisfactorily explains why languages are vulnerable to change only on the assumption that the strong version of the thesis of the Arbitrariness of the Sign discussed earlier – and *inter alia* of

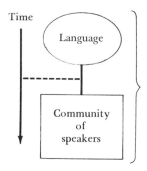

Figure 3.2

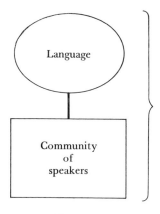

Figure 3.3

the Autonomy of Language – has been established, which it clearly has not been; and that even then it is only an explanation of why they are vulnerable, not of why in fact they change.

In conclusion, Saussure argues that to take account of the effects of the two most important factors introduced into the argument at this point, time and the social collective, we must represent *langue* as in Figure 3.2. This replaces the representation suggested by the earlier discussion, which, to take cognisance of the fact that *langue* is a social fact, exhibits its dependence on the linguistic community (fig. 3.3). What is inadequate about this representation is that it ignores historical factors. But to do this is to ignore something of crucial importance, for

the thing which keeps language from being a simple convention
that can be modified at the whim of the interested parties is not
its social nature; it is rather the action of time combined with the
social force. If time is left out, the linguistic facts are incomplete
and no conclusion is possible. (*CLG*, 113, 78)

But now that questions about the importance of historical issues
have been raised, the time has come to see what methodological
implications they have, and it is to these that Saussure now turns.
In so doing he introduces the second major dichotomy of *CLG*,
that between synchronic and diachronic linguistics – a topic
which forms the subject matter of our next chapter.

3.5. Summary

Saussure was root and branch opposed to nomenclaturism, the
view that a language consists of names whose function is to label
independently identifiable objects or ideas. In opposition to this
view, he insists that a language is a system of signs, and that the
signifying features of a sign depend on its intralinguistic relations
to other signs belonging to the same system rather than on its
extralinguistic relations to pre-existing objects or ideas. Clearly,
two key ideas need development and expansion, that of a sign
and that of a system, and it is with the first of these that this
chapter was concerned.

A sign is, for Saussure, a 'two-sided entity' consisting of the
union of a signifier and a signified. A signifier is an acoustic
image, so that, for example, the signifier of the word 'cat' is not
the sound made when it is pronounced, but an image of the
sound; it is thus a psychological entity. A signified is initially
identified with the concept associated with the signifier, but this
identification, I argued, is potentially confusing; we should treat
it at best as provisional and await Saussure's considered expli-
cation of it as a value arising from a system (6.1).

One primordial principle governing signs maintains that they
are radically arbitrary. This is so because they are unmotivated.
There is nothing about the world which makes one signifier any
more appropriate for its signified than any other. Saussure dis-
cusses two apparent counterexamples, onomatopoeia and interjections, and has no difficulty in showing that these are not
serious counterexamples to the principle. However, he does not

raise, let alone discuss, other counterexamples which are theoretically much more important, so his arguments for the principle of the Arbitrariness of the Sign are, at this stage anyway, quite inadequate.

A second primordial principle concerns signifiers. It maintains that since what a signifier represents is auditory, it can only represent a span of time, which has a linear character – hence the name of the principle, the Linearity of the Signifier. Though much less discussed than the principle of the Arbitrariness of the Sign, this principle is, in Saussure's view, equally important, since 'the whole mechanism of language depends on it' (*CLG*, 103, 70). He thought that this is so, I argued, because without appeal to the principle of Linearity, his account of the way in which a language is constituted by a system of syntagmatic and associative relations would be powerless to answer the question of why these and only these types of relations constitute a language (5.3). However, I argued that the Linearity principle is far too strong from Saussure's point of view, since it implies that the only features that signifiers can represent are ones of temporal succession. It thus excludes the very possibility of associative relations, which are non-temporal by definition.

Discussion of the question of why languages are both mutable and immutable introduces a new and important dimension into the discussion: time. There are, Saussure argues, many reasons why languages should be resistant to change. Their arbitrariness means that a debate whether to change them could have no rational basis; they are extremely complex, and only a few experts understand them; since everyone is a language user, there is the difficulty of getting everyone to change old habits. On top of all this, another factor must be taken into consideration: the effect of time. Language is inherited, so that we say 'man' and 'dog' simply because that is what our ancestors did; hence, changes have to contend with solidarity with our traditions and practices as well as the weight of the collectivity.

In view of all this, it might seem impossible for languages to change, yet they do. How is this possible? Saussure's answer to this question is much less detailed than was his answer to the question of why languages are stable. There is no review of the kinds of factors that might be responsible for change; instead we get an assertion that, whatever its nature, change can only have one kind of effect, a shift in the relationship of the signifier to the signified. Moreover, Saussure mentions only one factor which makes languages vulnerable to change: their arbitrariness. So his explanation of why languages are vulnerable to change is, by comparison with his explanation of why they are resistant to it, very thin indeed.

Finally, having introduced the topic of time and stressed its importance, Saussure is faced with the question of what theoretical distinctions are called for by the study of linguistic change. This leads him to introduce the second great dichotomy, that between synchronic and diachronic linguistics; this is the topic of the next chapter.

4

LANGUAGE AS A SYSTEM
OF SIGNS
II: Diachronic and synchronic linguistics

Discussion of the factors which explain the mutability and immutability of language led to awareness of the importance of time. But few people have suspected, Saussure argues, that an adequate treatment of the effect of time calls for a radical distinction between two branches of linguistics, synchronic and diachronic linguistics.

At first sight, this second great dichotomy of *CLG* is much easier to grasp than the first, that between *langue* and *parole,* in that it seems to involve no more than a distinction, created by one's point of view, between studying a thing as it changes through time and studying it at a moment in time (Amacker 1975, 56). But though the first of the explanations Saussure himself gives of the distinction perhaps suggests a view like this, in the course of subsequent discussion he elaborates a distinction which is much more complicated and which involves criteria that are not just temporal.

It also becomes clear in the course of this elaboration why the relatively straightforward account given above of the distinction will not do from Saussure's point of view. For it implies that the subject matter of the two branches of linguistics is the same *thing* studied from different perspectives, whereas it is a cardinal point of Saussure's developed theory that this is not so. Synchronic linguistics studies *langue*, which is a system that is psychologically real, whereas diachronic linguistics is concerned with relations of succession between *individual items*, which speakers are unaware of and which are in no sense systematic. In other words, the two branches of linguistics have quite different subject matters:

> *Synchronic linguistics* will be concerned with the logical and psychological relations that bind together coexisting terms and form a system in the collective mind of speakers.
> *Diachronic linguistics*, on the contrary, will study relations that bind together successive terms not perceived by the collective mind but substituted for each other without forming a system. (*CLG*, 140, 100)

This conception of diachronic linguistics throws down the gauntlet to nineteenth-century historical linguists by asserting that insofar as they are concerned only with historical questions, they are not concerned with language (*langue*) at all – hence Saussure's paradoxical dictum that 'there is no such thing as "historical grammar"; the discipline so labelled is really only diachronic linguistics' (*CLG*, 185, 134). In other words, Saussure claims, historical linguistics has nothing to do with grammar, which is the subject matter of synchronic linguistics; that of historical linguistics is quite other.

At first sight this dictum seems to be a root-and-branch rejection of the claims of historical linguistics; and this is indeed so, in the sense that Saussure believed that the methodologies and presuppositions of nineteenth-century historical linguistics were fundamentally flawed. But his critique of historical linguistics, though unquestionably severe, was not meant to be wholly negative or to lead to the conclusion that an interest in historical and comparative questions is improper. On the contrary, as well as severely criticising the existing methodology and assumptions of historical linguistics, he attempted to develop a methodology for investigating historical and comparative questions which was not vulnerable to the objections levelled against current practices. Indeed, the proposed new methodology for diachronic linguistics – which should not be confused with historical linguistics as it was currently practised – seems to rest on a plausible analysis of how one should analyse and explain change in something. This involves three steps:

(i) Describing its state at two different times t and t'

(ii) Comparing the two states to see in what respects the later state at t' differs from the earlier state at t

(iii) Identifying the causes of the differences between the two states

This approach would, of course, make the resolution of comparative and historical questions depend on synchronic analyses, since, applied to a language, step (i) of the analysis would call for two synchronic descriptions of different states of that language. Hence, synchronic questions are logically prior, so that without a satisfactory answer to them diachronic linguistics cannot even get off the ground. However, Saussure claims, the actual practice of the historical linguist has been like that of an artist who tries to produce a panorama of the Alps by viewing them from different peaks at the same time:

> The same applies to language; the linguist can neither describe it nor draw up standards of usage except by concentrating on one state. When he follows the evolution of the language, he resembles the moving observer who goes from one peak of the Jura to another in order to record the shifts in perspective. (*CLG*, 117, 82)

But, as we shall see, though Saussure developed a radical critique of historical linguistics as it was then practised, his attempt to develop an alternative methodology was inhibited by a number of theoretical assumptions which make it difficult to make sense of the idea that a language can change at all.

4.1. A science of pure values

Though consideration of the effects of time is Saussure's starting point, he concedes that many disciplines which take account of it do not need to split themselves up into two branches; astronomy, for instance, does not consist of synchronic astronomy and diachronic astronomy. In fact it is only sciences which are concerned with values that need to make a rigorous distinction

> between (1) *the axis of simultaneities* (AB), which stands for the relations of coexisting things and from which the intervention of time is excluded; and (2) *the axis of successions* (CD), on which only

one thing can be considered at a time but upon which are located
all the things on the first axis together with their changes.

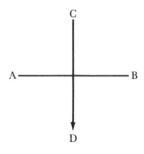

(*CLG*, 115, 80)

The reason why a concern with values calls for such a distinction
is, according to Saussure's own notes, because values always imply a system (Engler 2, 178). The implication is that values can
be studied only on the axis of simultaneities because there is
nothing systematic about change in their case.

Nevertheless, Saussure concedes that some values can be studied on both axes; for instance, since the value of a plot of land
is related to its productivity, we can trace its value through time
provided that 'we remember that its value depends at each moment upon a system of coexisting values' (*CLG*, 116, 80). Saussure's thought here seems to be that it is not unreasonable to
postulate some relationship between changes in productivity and
changes in value, so that if these do not form a system they are
nevertheless systematic.

But even if this is correct, the case of linguistics is different.
What makes it different from economics is, Saussure argues, the
fact that whilst economic values are not purely arbitrary, linguistic values are. Because this is so, language is a system of pure
values 'determined by nothing except the momentary arrangement of its terms' (ibid.).[1] Moreover, the sheer complexity of
language, one of the facts mentioned to explain its relative stability (3.4.1), compels one to study it separately on each of the
two coordinates distinguished above.

After considering various names for these two different studies, Saussure opts for 'synchronic linguistics' as the name of the
study which describes linguistic phenomena on the axis of simultaneities, and 'diachronic linguistics' for the other study,

which is concerned with the evolution of languages. But these explanations are, to say the least, underdetermined. Though it is clear that synchronic linguistics is concerned with systems of values in ways in which diachronic linguistics is not, and that the latter is concerned with evolution, not simply with change, whilst the former is not, the precise differences between the subject matter and methodology of the two sciences are at this point very unclear. Moreover, since the two axes cross, one could be forgiven for assuming that what we are dealing with is one and the same thing studied from two different points of view, which is, as we saw, certainly not what Saussure believes (Harris 1987, 89).

Before moving on to examples that Saussure gives to illustrate the differences between the two sciences, three aspects of his argument so far are worthy of comment. First, the claim that linguistics differs from other sciences concerned with values by being concerned with *pure* values rests on a much stronger version of the autonomy of language than the arguments about the arbitrariness of the sign have produced to date (3.2). For whilst we are left to glean what exactly is the difference between a pure value and other values, the root idea seems to be that whereas the latter are at least partially determined by factors external to the system to which they belong, the former is not. So if Saussure's account of the linguistic sign is correct, the values associated with it would be pure ones precisely because the sign is radically arbitrary, that is unmotivated (3.2). However, as we saw, Saussure's argument to show that linguistic signs are radically arbitrary fails to show that this is indeed so.

Second, it is not immediately clear why, even if the values in question are pure ones, Saussure should not concede that linguistics can study them 'historically', at least to the extent that economics can, by comparing the synchronically determined value of something at one time with its synchronically determined value at another; that is, by employing the method of analysing and explaining change outlined above.

The final point is connected with this: that in differentiating the historical study of economic values from that of linguistic values, Saussure comes very close to maintaining that there is no such thing as the history of changes of the latter, and *a fortiori* no such thing as the history of changes in a language. For if linguistic values are determined only by the momentary arrangement of terms, there cannot be any systematic factors which explain why one arrangement succeeds another. If there were, then linguistic values would be determined by more than the momentary arrangements in question. But even if such a view is ultimately defensible, it is surely surprising.

4.2. Differences between synchronic and diachronic facts

One important difference between synchronic and diachronic facts is that the succession of the facts of language 'in time does not exist insofar as the speaker is concerned. He is confronted with a state' (*CLG*, 171, 81). In other words, whilst the current state of their language is psychologically real for speakers, its history is not. For instance, as Culler points out, the French noun *pas* (step) and the negative adverb *pas* (not) have a common origin, but

> this is irrelevant to a description of modern French, where the two words function in totally different ways and must be treated as distinct signs. It makes no difference to modern French whether these two signs were once, as is in fact the case, a single sign, or whether they were once totally distinct signs whose different signifiers have become similar through sound changes. (1976, 37)

So it is the present state of the language which determines for the speaker whether there are one or two signs to be considered, not the history of the signs themselves, of which most speakers can be presumed to know nothing. We must distinguish those facts which are psychologically real for speakers and which determine values from those which are not and do not.

An example Saussure uses to illustrate these and other differences between the two species of fact is the following. In modern English there are a number of nouns of which the plural is marked by a specific vowel change – 'foot:feet', 'tooth:teeth', 'goose:geese', etc. That is a fact about contemporary English, which is psychologically real for speakers in that they will recognise the second member of each of the pairs above as the plural of the first member. But the history of how these nouns came to mark their plurals in this way is, Saussure points out, very complicated, involving three previous stages:

Stage 1	*Stage 2*	*Stage 3*
fōt:fōti	*fōt:fēti*	*fōt:fēt*
tōþ:tōþi	*tōþ:tēþi*	*tōþ:tēþ*
gōs:gōsi	*gōs:gēsi*	*gōs:gēs*

In the first of these stages, Anglo-Saxon, the plural was marked by a final *i*, a claim which is part of a synchronic description of that language state. Then, as a result of a phonetic change (not limited to this class of nouns; it occurred whenever *i* followed a stressed syllable [Culler 1976, 43]), the forms listed in Stage 2 evolved. In this stage, as in the first, the plural is still marked by a final *i*, but it is also marked by the contrast between *o* and *e*. Then another phonetic change occurred that led to the dropping of the final *i* (a change which, again, was not restricted to these cases). The result of this second change was Stage 3, in which there is only one way of marking the plural, viz. by means of the contrast between *o* and *e*. Our modern forms result from Stage 3 as a result of the great vowel shift.

Now, Saussure argues, not only is the evolution of the modern form complicated, but it is necessary when describing that evolution to distinguish sharply descriptions of how the plural is formed in any given state, which are synchronic descriptions, from descriptions of the factors which have led to the evolution of one form from another:

The relation between a singular and a plural, whatever the forms may be, can be expressed at each moment by a horizontal axis:

Whatever facts have brought about passage from one form to another should be placed along a vertical axis, giving the overall picture:

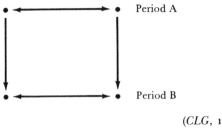

Period A

Period B

(*CLG*, 120, 84)

Moreover, Saussure argues, the diachronic facts responsible for the transition from Stage 1 to Stage 3 were not directed to bringing that transition about. The phonetic changes involved in the transition from Stage 1 to Stage 2, for instance, had nothing specifically to do with the plural, since they involved all cases in which an *i* followed a stressed syllable. It just so happened that as a result the language contained forms which marked the plural in two different ways, both by the addition of *i* and by the contrast between *o* and *e*.

This point illustrates one of Saussure's crucial principles about change, namely that *changes never modify language states directly.* That is, they have effects on certain items, which may then affect the system, but if the system is modified it is always modified indirectly. A change in the mass of one of the planets is an example of an isolated event which 'would throw the whole system out of equilibrium' (*CLG*, 121, 85). An isolated change occurs which as such is not a change in the system; but indirectly the system is affected. Analogously, the dropping of the final *i* which led to Stage 3 is an example of a change in an element in a system which indirectly affects the whole system, i.e., leaves only one way of signalling the plural in the nouns in question. Because changes do not affect the system itself, but only one or some of its elements, they can, Saussure concludes, be studied only outside the system.

But if a language state is the result of changes which were not directed to bringing it about, then it must be fortuitous: 'In a fortuitous state (*fōt:fēt*), speakers took advantage of an existing difference and made it signal the distinction between singular and plural; *fōt:fēt* is no better for this purpose than *fōt:fōti*. In each state the mind infiltrated a given substance and breathed life into it' (*CLG*, 122, 85). It follows, Saussure claims, that synchronic and diachronic facts are very different:

Diachronic facts	Synchronic facts
Not concerned with values	Concerned with values
Not intentional; the systematic changes produced are not designed	Speakers 'breathe life' into differences[2]
Involve only one term; the new one, *fēt*, replaces the old, *fōti*	Involve two terms; the opposition between *fōt* and *fēt* expresses the plural
Not systematic	Systematic

Strictly speaking, of course, change may involve more than one term. What is crucial from Saussure's point of view is that it is not systematic, so that the terms involved are in that sense isolated terms.

Saussure's claim that the values of a sign in a particular language state do not depend on facts about its history is one that has come to be widely accepted. So too has the first of the arguments he uses, namely the epistemological argument that facts which are unknown to speakers cannot determine the significance of what they say. However, since speakers are often aware of changes in their language, the argument is not strong enough to rule out all historical influences; for that, an additional argument is needed. Further, Saussure's principle that changes never modify language states directly seems to exclude dogmatically the possibility of factors present in a given state precipitating a change which results in a new state. If this was indeed possible, then the successive states would have a more intimate relationship than the merely contingent connection between successive states which is all that is possible on Saussure's own account. As things stand, because of his view that change is neither precipitated by, nor directly affects, a language state, Saussure's position is one which makes it difficult to make sense of the idea that languages change at all. For if successive states are not related to each other systematically, then it is difficult to see what makes them states of the same language rather than simply different language states (4.3).

But before considering these issues in more detail, we must first consider a powerful and persuasive analogy which Saussure develops to illustrate the contrast and the differences, methodological and otherwise, that he sees between the two branches of linguistics.

4.3. Language and the game of chess

Many different and conflicting metaphors and analogies are employed in *CLG* to illuminate the nature of language. Perhaps the most influential is one of three analogies developed by Saussure to illustrate the distinction between synchronic and diachronic linguistics: the comparison with a game of chess.[3]

The comparison is, Saussure says, the most illuminating, because in both cases we are confronted with systems of values: 'A game of chess is like an artificial realization of what language offers in a natural form' (*CLG*, 125, 88). He does not expand on this claim, but presumably what he has in mind is the fact that to learn how to play chess someone has to learn what the point of the game is, what the relative weights of the pieces are, and what their legitimate moves are. Moreover, none of these things would seem to be determined by external exigencies or designed to achieve an ulterior purpose; they are internal to the game in the sense that they depend on the nature of the game itself and nothing else. So if the pieces in a game have a value, or weight, they would seem to be paradigm examples of pure values (4.1).

There are three main points of comparison seen by Saussure between chess and a language. First, just as in a given state of the game the value of a piece depends on its position on the board, and *a fortiori* on its relations to the other pieces, so in a given language state the value of a word depends on its relations to other words in that state. Second, since any given state is momentary, the value of a piece varies from state to state; the same is true of language states and words. Third, in a chess game only one piece has to be moved to pass from one state to another. This is a strict counterpart of the phenomena studied by diachronic linguistics in a number of respects: In language too, change affects only 'isolated elements'. Nevertheless, in both cases the move has repercussions for the whole system. In chess an actual move is part of neither the preceding nor the succeeding system; it links them. Only states matter: '... the route used in arriving there makes absolutely no difference; one who has followed the entire match has no advantage over the curious party who comes up at a critical time to inspect the state of the game' (*CLG*, 127, 89). The same is true of a language: 'Speaking (*parole*) operates only on a language state, and the changes that intervene between states have no place in either state' (ibid.).

Of course no analogy is perfect, and there is, Saussure concedes, one important respect in which a game of chess differs from a language. For whereas the moves made in chess are designed to bring about the resulting states, linguistic changes are not so designed, so that the states that result are purely fortuitous. But this makes the need for a complete distinction between synchrony and diachrony in the case of language even more urgent: 'For if diachronic facts cannot be reduced to the synchronic system which they condition when the change is intentional, all the more will they resist when they set a blind force against the organization of a system of signs' (ibid.). But this apart, the analogy is in Saussure's view exact.

There might indeed also seem to be another important difference, namely that in a game of chess, even if the values of pieces change from move to move, nevertheless the same rules of the game remain in force in succeeding states – this is what makes the successive states ones belonging to the same game. Thus, however powerful a piece it is in a given state, a bishop can move only along the diagonal. So some part of the value of a piece in successive states remains constant. But on Saussure's own account it is hard to see what could be analogous in the case of a language to the rules of chess; that is, it is hard to see what could be operative in a similar way in successive states of the language. And because this is so, it is difficult to see what reason there is on Saussure's account for treating successive states as ones of the same language (4.2).

In the course of making his second point, that the value of a piece changes from state to state, Saussure tries to meet this objection: 'Rules that are agreed on once and for all exist in language too; they are the constant principles of semiology' (*CLG*, 126, 88). But apart from the fact that he once again draws a blank cheque on a non-existent science, the comparison is clearly wrong. The rules of semiology, if they existed, would constrain all sign systems; what would correspond to them in the case of chess would be not its own rules but the rules of any possible game. So even if there are rules of semiology, they do not stand to particular language states as do the rules of chess to successive states of a game. This disanalogy is, as I have urged, serious, because it leaves us with no account of how we identify successive states as states of the same language, or indeed of how we decide what to include within them or to exclude; in other words, what to count as one state[4] (Harris 1987, 93).

There are various other disanalogies or awkwardnesses in the comparison, of which two are important. First, it is not really true, as Saussure claims, that in chess each state of the game is independent of all antecedent states. Various things will tell the casual observer that a game has been going on for a long or short time; for example, missing pieces and the placement of others on the board. In other words, the history of the game, though obviously not recoverable in detail, will not be completely opaque.[5] Second, and perhaps more important, the acute observer will be able to perceive various strategic possibilities in a given state and speculate intelligently about what moves will come next.

Perhaps Saussure's answer to this point would be that the fact that this is so is simply a consequence of the fact that in chess the players intend to produce the resulting states, and that this is just another respect in which a game of chess and a language diverge. However, such a response, as well as underscoring the extent of the differences that flow from the admitted one,[6] would further emphasise the point that there is a total lack of connection on Saussure's account between successive language states.

The third disanalogy is that whilst there is no theoretical problem in the case of chess in distinguishing on a temporal continuum between successive states and the moves that produce them, there is a problem in distinguishing between successive language states and the changes that produce them. In the following, S, S', etc. are states, and M, M', etc. moves in a game of chess.

$$
\begin{array}{ccc}
[& S^n &] \\
[& M^{n-1} &] \\
& \cdots & \\
& \cdots & \\
[& M^2 &] \\
[& S^2 &]
\end{array}
$$

$$[\quad M' \quad]$$
$$[\quad S' \quad]$$

The different states may of course last for differing periods of time – as long in fact as the player whose turn it is takes to make his next move. But the moment he makes his move a new state comes into being, and the time taken to make the move has no significance, so that the transition from one state to another is in effect instantaneous. Hence, at any given time the game is in some determinate state or other, and it is, moreover, clear what belongs to that state and what does not. Now, if the analogy with a language were exact, then it too could be analysed neatly into successive language states, and the time taken to effect the transition – to make the linguistic move, as it were – could be ignored. But in fact transitional periods may last a considerable time, during which there is no uniform practice in the area subject to change, e.g., the way in which the plural is marked. So what should be said about such periods?

We shall return to this issue later; the point to note now is that the model of change suggested by the analogy with chess is a much more complicated one than the original one involving only the axes of succession and simultaneity.

4.4. The two linguistics

Since, on Saussure's view, synchronic and diachronic linguistics have different objects, it is not surprising that he should maintain that they have different methodologies. In particular he stresses two major differences, and in the course of doing so further deepens the characterisation of the terms 'synchronic' and 'diachronic' in ways which underscore the point made at the end of the preceding section: that the original model involving the axes of simultaneity and succession is too simple for his purposes.

The first major difference is the evidential basis of the two branches of linguistics. Synchronic linguistics is concerned only with what is psychologically real for the members of a linguistic community, presumably at a given time, so that 'to know just to what extent a thing is a reality, it is necessary and sufficient to determine to what extent it exists in the minds of speakers' (CLG, 128, 90). But in diachronic linguistics there is no such restriction. It has two perspectives: 'One of these, the *prospective*, follows the

course of time; the other, the *retrospective,* goes back in time'
(ibid.). In other words, diachronic linguistics is in no way restricted to facts which are psychologically real for a given community of speakers.

The second big difference is that synchronic linguistics is concerned only with the 'totality of facts corresponding to each
language; separation will go as far as dialects and subdialects
when necessary' (ibid.). In other words, a synchronic study is
concerned not with all simultaneously existing facts but only with
subsets of these, namely those belonging to one language. Thus,
Saussure says, strictly speaking we should talk not of synchronic
linguistics but of *idiosynchronic* linguistics.

By contrast, diachronic linguistics is not similarly restricted;
'the terms that it studies do not necessarily belong to the same
language (compare Proto-Indo-European *esti*, Greek *esti*, German *ist*, and French *est*)' (*CLG*, 129, 90). Indeed, as Saussure's
example makes clear, not only is diachronic linguistics not confined to one language, it is not even necessary for the terms
compared to be in use at different times, as is clear from the
reference to German *ist* and French *est*. This is so because 'to
justify the associating of two forms, it is enough to show that
they are connected by a historical bond, however indirect it may
be' (*CLG*, 129, 91). So the fact that a modern German word and
a modern French word have a common origin is a diachronic
fact.

It should now be clear just how inadequate the original model
of the distinction between the two linguistics, with its two temporal axes, has become. For synchronic linguistics is concerned
not with all simultaneously existing facts but only with what is
idiosynchronic, whilst items which are of interest to diachronic
linguistics may be in use at the same time.

Moreover, if Saussure's explanations of the terms of the dichotomy are to be applicable, he must have available some independent characterisation of a language. Otherwise, it is hard
to see how, when asked what synchronic linguistics studies, he
could avoid giving the answer 'The state of a language'. But
when asked how one identifies this, the only answer hinted at
in these passages is that it is something that is psychologically
real at a given time for a community of speakers. However, since
there may be many different things which have this status –

imagine a bilingual community, for instance – the explanation will come to a premature full stop at this point unless we are given a characterisation of what it is for a language to be a shared language of the community.

4.4.1. No panchronic viewpoint

Given the differences in both subject matter and methodology of the two branches of linguistics, it is hardly surprising that Saussure concludes that there is no panchronic viewpoint, at least as far as what he calls 'concrete' entities are concerned. Concrete entities are the signs that constitute a language, and they are, according to Saussure, 'not abstractions but real objects' (*CLG*, 144, 102).[7] For instance, if we take a word, the French word *chose*, for instance, there is no point of view which combines both the diachronic perspective, in which 'it stands in opposition to the Latin word from which it derives, *causa*', and the synchronic perspective, in which 'it stands in opposition to every word that might be associated with it in Modern French' (*CLG*, 135, 95). The sounds produced when the word is spoken can of course be studied from a panchronic viewpoint, but they have no linguistic value – a claim which follows from what Saussure said about the French word *nu* (2.1).

Saussure's denial of a panchronic viewpoint was, as we saw, qualified; there is no such viewpoint as far as concrete entities are concerned. Does that mean that in the case of what are in Saussure's view abstract entities (cases and parts of speech, for instance) there is a panchronic viewpoint? Clearly not, for '*abstract entities are always based, in the last analysis, on concrete entities*' (*CLG*, 190, 138). Instead, what Saussure has in mind when he admits the existence of a panchronic viewpoint are the unchanging principles of semiology: 'In linguistics as in chess there are rules that outlive all events. But they are general principles existing independently of concrete facts' (*CLG*, 135, 95). For example, on Saussure's account any language must consist of a number of signs which stand in both syntagmatic and associative relation to each other (5.3). That is true of all languages at all times. But, his point seems to be, this tells us nothing at all about what signs there actually are in any given language.

4.5. The second bifurcation

The introduction of the dichotomy between synchronic and diachronic linguistics leads us to the second great bifurcation. The first was, of course, that between *langue* and *parole*. But how are the two dichotomies related? A diagram is introduced to illustrate 'the rational form that linguistic study should take.'

$$
\text{(Human) Speech}
\begin{cases}
\text{Language}
\begin{cases}
\text{Synchrony} \\
\text{Diachrony}
\end{cases} \\
\text{Speaking}
\end{cases}
$$

(*CLG*, 139, 98)

But the diagram is something of a puzzle. It suggests that there could be both a synchronic and a diachronic study of *langue*, whilst *parole* itself is left completely out in the cold as the subject matter of neither branch of linguistics.

It is even harder to avoid the conclusion that as a summary of the preceding discussion the diagram is quite misleading when it is viewed in the light of the remark, on the same page, that 'everything diachronic in language is diachronic only by virtue of speaking (*parole*)' (ibid.). This is so, Saussure argues, because the germ of all change is to be found in *parole*:

> Each change is launched by a certain number of individuals before it is accepted for general use. Modern German uses *ich war, wir waren*, whereas until the sixteenth century the conjugation was *ich was, wir waren* (cf. English *I was, we were*). How did the substitution of *war* for *was* come about? Some speakers, influenced by *waren*, created *war* through analogy; this was a fact of speaking (*parole*); the new form, repeated many times and accepted by the community, became a fact of language. (Ibid.)

Interestingly, this account describes change on the model outlined at the beginning of this chapter. There is a synchronic description of the initial language state, sixteenth-century German, and one of the state that succeeded it, modern German. And there is a description of the mechanism by which the change occurred. Seizing on an analogy, some speakers produced a variant which was, as such, of no intrinsic interest. But when the variant became the norm, so to speak, it became part of the language, with the result that *war* was substituted for *was*. Of course, not all variants are successful, and as long as 'they remain individual, they may be ignored, for we are studying language' (ibid.). Thus, on this account a diachronic study incorporates a number of synchronic descriptions as well as an account of the way in which they are related by facts of speech; that is, a diachronic study is not just a study of *langue*, it is a study also of *parole*. This is necessary, because it is only by reference to the latter that an account of the mechanism of change can be given. So it is hard to see how *parole* can be excluded from the subject matter of diachronic linguistics.

Moreover, this example of Saussure's highlights certain tensions in his overall account. For the fact that *war* was substituted for *was* by analogy strongly suggests that the state of German itself plays a part in the account of change. There existed a potential for that change in the shape of an imitable model: 'Analogy supposes a model and its regular imitation. *An analogical form is form made on the model of one or more other forms in accordance with a definite rule*' (*CLG*, 221, 161). But if language states have such a potential, in the form of so-called productive forms, it seems hard to maintain that successive language states always have the strict independence of each other that Saussure's theory requires.[8]

Saussure's implied answer to this objection is characteristically bold: He denies that in such cases there is any change. On the contrary, what we have is a case of creation of a new form. One proof that this is properly described as creation rather than change is the fact that the old form remains unchanged, and, for a time anyway, the two subsist side by side.

But this response, taken seriously, might well force him to maintain that there is never any change; for in the only other kind of change he recognises, phonetic change, it is perfectly possible for individual variants of a standard form to coexist with it before ultimately replacing it. The principle that a system can change only if some part of it has changed would seem to be far too strong if cases in which variants or analogical creations, which initially coexist with original forms but ultimately replace them, are not counted as examples of changes in the original forms.

4.6. Summary and prospect

A central question raised by our discussion is which of the two
conceptions of change developed by Saussure is the preferred
one. As we saw, the model of change implicit in the chess analogy
is more complicated than the original one involving only the
intersection of the two temporal axes (4.1). Moreover, it became
clear – in the light of Saussure's claim that synchronic linguistics
is, strictly speaking, concerned with what is idiosynchronic, whilst
usages in existence at the same time can be of interest to diachronic linguistics – that the distinction between a synchronic
and a diachronic study involves more than the temporal considerations involved in the original model. This suggests that the
model implicit in the chess analogy is the preferred one. One
advantage of the latter model is that it certainly allows one to
take into consideration the fact that language states may be of
longer or shorter durations, for players make their moves more
rapidly at some times than at others. As Saussure says,

> It is possible for a language to change hardly at all over a long
> span and then to undergo radical transformations within a few
> years. Of two languages that exist side by side during a given
> period, one may evolve drastically and the other practically not
> at all. (*CLG*, 142, 101)

Even so, I argued that the chess model highlights a serious problem. In chess, the moment a player makes his move a new state
of the board comes into being, and the time taken actually to
make the move has no significance. Hence, the transition from
one state to another is in effect instantaneous, so that at any
given time the game is in some determinate state or other. Now,
if the analogy with a language were exact, then the language
could be analysed neatly into successive language states, and the
time taken to effect a transition could be ignored. But clearly
this is not so, since a transitional period may last for a considerable time, during which there is no uniform practice in the
area subject to change.

Saussure's implicit solution to the problem posed by the disanalogy is clear. In the case of two languages, one of which is
evolving rapidly and the other not, 'study would have to be
diachronic in the former instance, synchronic in the latter' (ibid.).

In other words, successive language states, which can be studied synchronically, do not necessarily succeed each other immediately; there may intervene periods of change which can only be the subject of a diachronic study. Reverting to the chess analogy, this would be to treat the time taken to make a move as of significance, so that whilst the move is being made the game is not in any particular state at all (Harris 1987, 105). But the implications of what is said at this point are, to say the least, difficult to reconcile with Saussure's overall position. For surely if there are times at which a synchronic description of a language is not possible, then it is hard to see what a description of the *langue* internalised by its speakers could be. But one of Saussure's central claims is that without *langue* there can be no *parole*. So if no synchronic description of a language is possible, it is hard to see how, on his principles, there could be a diachronic one either.

Further, Saussure writes as though the conception of a stable state is, at best, a methodological fiction: '... since language changes somewhat in spite of everything, studying a language-state means in practice disregarding changes of little importance, just as mathematicians disregard infinitesimal quantities in certain calculations, such as logarithms' (*CLG*, 142, 101). But fiction or not, the assumption that there are such states, which, moreover, form the subject matter of synchronic linguistics, seems to be central to Saussure's thought. However, it is far from clear that he succeeded in developing a satisfactory model which differentiates the subject matter of synchronic linguistics from that of diachronic linguistics. Certainly the original model involving only the two temporal axes is inadequate, whilst the analogy with chess, which forms the basis for Saussure's preferred model, limps badly at a number of points.

We shall return to some of these issues in Chapter 7. But we must now turn to Saussure's detailed account of the way in which a language constitutes a very special kind of system, one of pure values.

5

LANGUAGE AS A SYSTEM OF SIGNS
III: Identities, system, and relations

Synchronic linguistics, it will be recalled, is 'concerned with the logical and psychological relations that bind together co-existing terms and form a system in the collective minds of speakers' (*CLG*, 140, 99). Such a system is, Saussure claims, one of pure values. But why must linguistic terms belong to such a system? What are the relations which relate them to each other? And why is a system of terms which are related to each other by these relations one of pure values? Saussure's answer to the first two questions is the principal subject matter of this chapter; Chapter 6 is devoted to discussion of the third. Hence in these two chapters we shall trace the way in which Saussure's answers to these questions lead to the conclusion that 'a linguistic system is a series of differences of sound combined with a series of differences of ideas' the combination of which 'engenders a system of values'; moreover, 'this system serves as the effective link between the phonic and the psychological elements within each sign' (*CLG*, 166, 120). But before we consider the detailed argument, I shall begin by raising what is at first sight a rather curious question: What precisely are the terms of the system in question?

5.1. Concrete and abstract entities

The question seems curious, because in the light of the previous discussion the answer appears to be obvious: They are linguistic signs. But granted that that is so, why is it important from Saussure's point of view to insist that 'the signs that make up language are not abstractions but real objects (see p. 15); signs and their relations are what linguistics studies; they are the *concrete entities* of our science' (*CLG*, 144, 102)? In other words, what is the point of insisting that the entities we are dealing with are real and concrete?

Part of the answer is that, considered in isolation, signifiers and signifieds are not linguistic entities: 'A succession of sounds is linguistic only if it supports an idea.... The same is true of the signified as soon as it is separated from its signifier' (*CLG*, 144, 103). So from the point of view of linguistics, signifiers and signifieds considered in isolation are abstractions, which is not to say, of course, that they are abstract entities.

But the roots of Saussure's insistence that the entities in question are concrete go deeper than this. The problems that he grapples with derive from the second of his primordial principles, namely the Linear Nature of the Signifier (3.3). This principle, it will be recalled, maintains that the elements of auditory signifiers 'are presented in succession; they form a chain' (*CLG*, 103, 70). In other words, the principle tells us that if such a signifier as [onehundredandone] is complex, so that there is a question of what its constituent signifiers are, we can rule out such *a priori* possibilities as that its constituent signifiers can co-occur or be discontinuous.[1] According to the principle, however a complex sign is to be segmented, the resulting units must be distinct both from what precedes them and from what succeeds them in the chain. Hence Saussure's claim that 'the linguistic entity is not accurately defined until it is *delimited*, i.e. separated from everything that surrounds it on the phonic chain. These delimited entities or units stand in opposition to each other in the mechanism of language' (*CLG*, 145, 103). But how is this delimiting to be done? The discussion of *nu* earlier (2.1) made it clear that any attempt to delimit a linguistic unit in purely physical terms would lack a rationale. For there would be indefinitely many ways of segmenting any sequence in which *nu* occurred. But is it not possible that, whatever criterion we use, there is more than one way of carrying out the analysis into segments? In other words, is it not possible that there is a radical indeterminacy in the procedure envisaged (7.2)?

Saussure apparently thought not, provided that we appeal to meanings: 'Considered by itself, it [the signifier] is only a line, a continuous ribbon along which the ear perceives no self-sufficient and clear-cut division; to divide the chain we must call in meanings' (ibid.). So, for instance, a reason for accepting [hundred] as a signifier would be that it corresponds to a signified, whereas [andone] does not. It follows that the kind of unit of interest to linguistics 'has no special phonic character, and the only definition that we can give it is this: it is *a slice of sound which to the exclusion of everything that precedes and follows it in the spoken chain is the signifier of a certain concept*' (*CLG*, 146, 104). Moreover, Saussure goes on to describe a method of linguistic analysis which commends itself in the light of this discussion:

> One who knows a language singles out its units by a very simple method – in theory, at any rate. His method consists of using speaking as the source material of language and picturing it as two parallel chains, one of concepts (A) and the other of sound-images (B).
>
> In an accurate delimitation, the division along the chain of sound-images (*a, b, c*) will correspond to the division along the chain of concepts (*a', b', c'*):

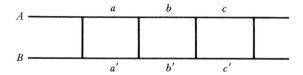

> Take French *sižlaprā*. Can we cut the chain after *l* and make *sižl* a unit? No, we need only consider the concepts to see that the division is wrong. (*CLG*, 146, 104)

In fact, Saussure goes on to argue, there are only two possible divisions, both of which are determined by the meaning expressed by the words: *si-ž-la-prā* and *si-ž-l-aprā* – respectively, *si je la prends* ('if I take it') and *si je l'apprends* ('if I learn it').

One obvious consequence of this proposal is that concrete

units, whatever they are, cannot be identified with words. Some units will be only parts of words – 'painful', for instance, can be segmented into two elements, 'pain' and 'ful', each of which clearly has meaning – whilst others will be longer than a word – for instance, idioms, such as 'kick the bucket'.

But if a concrete unit is a slice of sound which signifies a certain concept, what is an abstract unit and what makes it abstract? The examples Saussure gives include word order (e.g., 'pain-ful' is possible, but not '*ful-pain'), case and case endings, and parts of speech. Since, for instance, a concrete unit may be a noun but cannot itself be identified with the category *noun*, no part of the speech chain can be identified with the category. Hence, the latter is not concrete and so has to be treated as abstract, as do case endings and cases, for similar reasons.

However, Saussure seems to have had more in mind than this when he called units abstract, namely a doubt whether so-called abstract entities are psychologically real. Their study is, he says, difficult, 'because we never know exactly whether or not the awareness of speakers goes as far as the analysis of the grammarian. But the important thing is that *abstract entities are always based, in the last analysis, on concrete entities*' (*CLG*, 190, 138). In other words, another major difference between concrete and abstract entities is that whereas the former are psychologically real, it is possible that the latter are not. Hence the possibility that grammarians employ categories which are quite unfamiliar to native speakers.[2]

This difficulty apart, it seems that Saussure employs two different criteria to determine whether an entity is concrete. According to the first, as we have just seen, a concrete unity is psychologically real. But according to the second it must be delimitable in the speech chain in the way in which *la* is in *sižlaprā* (*SM*, 210); and it is this criterion to which the method for singling out units that we described appeals. But though the method is 'very simple in theory' (*CLG*, 147, 105), there are, Saussure points out, difficulties in applying it in practice. For instance, though it is tempting to treat words as concrete units, this would not be correct: 'To be convinced; we need only think of French *cheval* 'horse' and its plural form *chevaux*. People readily say they are two forms of the same word; but considered as wholes, they are certainly two distinct things with respect to both meaning and sound' (*CLG*, 147, 105).

However, if people do see two forms of the same word when there are in fact two distinct concrete units, then arguably the two criteria pull in different directions. And whether or not this is so, one can see the practical difficulty of applying Saussure's method by asking which if any of the following are segmentable into two signifying constituents: [blackberry]/[blueberry]/[strawberry]/[cranberry]/[bilberry] ... As described, the method seems to be of little help in cases like this in which, confronted with the question whether or not [straw] is a significant constituent of [strawberry], one's intuitions are feeble.[3] Moreover, cases in which there is a conflict of intuitions – e.g., between two people one of whom wishes to segment *la* in *sižlaprā* into *l*, which signifies the pronominal third person, and *a*, which signifies the feminine gender, and the other who treats it as an unanalysed whole – clearly raise pertinent questions (Harris 1987, 109). How do we decide who is right?

Saussure's answer to this question is clear. After describing the procedure for analysing *sižlaprā*, he writes:

> To verify the result of the procedure and be assured that we are dealing with a unit, we must be able in comparing a series of sentences in which the same unit occurs to separate the unit from the rest of the context and find in each instance that meaning justifies that delimitation. Take two French phrases *laforsdüvā* (la *force* du vent 'the force of the wind'), and *abudufors* (a bout du *force* 'exhausted'; literally 'at the end of one's force'). In each phrase the same concept coincides with the same phonic slice *fors*; thus it is certainly a linguistic unit. But in *ilməforsaparle* (il me *force* à parler 'he *forces* me to talk') *fors* has an entirely different meaning: it is therefore another unit. (*CLG*, 146, 104)

This brings to the fore the question whether a given tranche of sound has the same meaning in different contexts; it is only if it has that it can be treated as a signifier, and the union of it and its associated meaning treated as a sign. In other words, it raises for Saussure the crucial question of synchronic identity; that is, of how we tell, for example, whether two occurrences of *fors* are constituents of the same sign. As we shall see, not only do Saussure's answers to the difficulties we have been discussing depend on his account of synchronic identity, but in order to give that account he has to explain the precise way in which signs form a system.

5.2. Why signs form a system

Saussure's answer to the question of synchronic identity has two parts. The first part consists of an argument to the effect that utter chaos would result if the effects of the principle of the Arbitrariness of the Sign were not restricted or diminished in some way. The second, and more important, tries to show that the identification of a particular signifier or signified depends on its belonging to a system, because, paradoxically, it is not any positive characteristic that it has which makes it what it is; what is important, rather, are the ways in which it differs from the other elements of the system. We must now consider each of these answers in turn.

5.2.1. Relative arbitrariness

Though a linguistic system is based on the principle of the Arbitrariness of the Sign, Saussure argues that it is a principle 'which would lead to the worst sort of complication if applied without restriction' (*CLG*, 182, 133). However, it is not in fact applied without restriction, since the mind 'contrives to introduce a principle of order and regularity into certain parts of the mass of signs' which is 'a partial correction of a system that is by nature chaotic' (ibid.). As a result, some signs, e.g., 'twenty-one', are said to be only relatively arbitrary, in contrast to those, like 'one', which are completely arbitrary.

Two characteristics mark a sign that is relatively arbitrary. It is complex and has a model. That is, it is constructed on the basis of a productive pattern, and because that is so, it necessarily involves a system. Thus, 'twenty-one', 'thirty-one', etc. are only relatively arbitrary, since they are constructed on a model, whereas 'three', since it has no model, is radically arbitrary. However, I argued earlier that to call the phenomenon relative arbitrariness is misleading, since the fact that a sign is constructed systematically does not make it less arbitrary than one that is not (3.2.1). In a metric system, 50p is just as much an arbitrary unit of money as 1p, even though it is part of a system. So system is not, as Saussure suggests, a degree of arbitrariness.

Indeed, Saussure's claim that if applied without restriction the principle of the Arbitrariness of the Sign would lead to the worst sort of complication, i.e., chaos, is something of an understatement if it suggests that we can conceive of a language that is not systematic. For any language that has a potential infinity of sentences must, if it is to be learnable, be systematic in a very precise sense; that is, it must be what Lyons calls productive. By this term he means 'that property of the language-system which enables native speakers to construct and understand an indefinitely large number of utterances, including utterances that they have never previously encountered' (1977, 76). The crucial importance of this property was, of course, first stressed by Chomsky (1957; 1965). So the task of linguistics is not simply to devise a description of a corpus of sentences, however large, but to describe the system knowledge of which enables native speakers to produce and understand indefinitely many sentences of their language.

The importance of system can, therefore, hardly be doubted; indeed, it is clearly of such crucial importance that it is difficult to see why, having recognised its importance, Saussure should not have seen the need to modify radically his claim that the principles of the Arbitrariness of the Sign and of the Linearity of the Signifier are the fundamental principles of a semiotic enquiry. For system is surely an independent principle, and not one that follows from the principles of arbitrariness and linearity, as he claims.

But if a language must be systematic, is it essential that every one of its signs belong to that system? A simple sign can, of course, occur as part of a complex sign, as does 'one' in 'twenty-one', and in that sense form part of a system. However, the argument so far has not shown either that, their occurrence in sentences apart, all simple signs do so occur or, more important, that to *identify* or define such a sign one has to know that it forms part of a system and what role it plays in that system. On the contrary, it might be argued that it is only if simple signs are independently identifiable and interpretable that the complex signs of which they form part are interpretable. If simple signs are not identifiable and interpretable independently of the other elements of the system to which they belong, then it is not obvious that they can be identified at all, for it is difficult to see how in that case anyone could master the system, since there is no point of entry to it.

So the fact that languages necessarily involve a system explains why many signs, viz. complex ones, can be identified and interpreted only by someone who has grasped the system. It also explains why, because they are systematically related to complex signs, there is a sense in which many, if not all, simple signs belong to a system. However, it does not show that simple signs too can be identified and interpreted only by someone who has grasped the system; and indeed the very idea that this is so runs counter to deeply held intuitions about the relation of the simple to the complex shared by philosophers as diverse as Locke, Leibniz, and Russell.

Nevertheless, Saussure certainly wants to argue that simple signs can only be so identified and interpreted. So, as it stands, the argument about the importance of system would seem to be insufficient for his purpose. What is needed at this point is an argument which shows that the identification of any sign, whether simple or complex, depends on the identification of a system of which it forms part.

5.2.2. Identities and differences

The crucial point that Saussure wants to make at this stage[4] is most clearly illustrated by his answer to the question of synchronic identity, the importance of which I stressed at the end of 5.1: In virtue of what can two occurrences of the same word be said to be the same? Suppose, for instance, that someone utters the word 'gentlemen' twice in the course of a speech, but with very different intonations on the two occasions. Why, in spite of all the differences there are between the separate speech events, do we recognise two occurrences of the same word? It can hardly be because of an absolute identity of the phonic substance on the two occasions, given the difference in emphasis and intonation; nor need there have been an 'absolute identity between one *Gentlemen!* and the next from the semantic viewpoint either' (*CLG*, 151, 108). What makes them the same, in spite of the differences, is the fact that there is one set of ways in which each of them differs from all the other words of the language. As for the admitted differences there are between them, these do not entail that they are not instances of the same word, any more than the myriad differences there are between two oak trees do not entail that they do not belong to the same species. In other words, some differences entail membership of different kinds, and others do not. If all did, then there would be no such thing as kind membership.

At this point Saussure develops an analogy:

> For instance, we speak of the identity of two '8:25 p.m. Geneva-to-Paris' trains that leave at twenty-four hour intervals. We feel that it is the same train every day, yet everything – the locomotive, coaches, personnel – is probably different.... what makes the express is its hour of departure, its route, and in general every circumstance that sets it apart from other trains. (*CLG*, 151, 108)

Saussure hastens to add that this does not make the train an abstract entity, since it must have a material realisation. Though there is no particular group of carriages and so forth that it must consist of, nevertheless it must consist of some. Thus the identity of the successive trains cannot be accounted for in terms of the material entities of which they are composed, for these might be completely different. What makes the two trains the same, in spite of their material differences, is the fact that each is related in the same way to a time of departure, a route, a set of connections with other trains, etc.

Another analogy that he develops to illustrate his point involves yet another comparison with chess:

> Take a knight, for instance. By itself is it an element in the game? Certainly not, for by its material make-up – outside its square and the other conditions of the game – it means nothing to the player; it becomes a real, concrete element only when endowed with value and wedded to it. Suppose that the piece happens to be destroyed or lost during a game. Can it be replaced by an equivalent piece? Certainly. (*CLG*, 153, 110)

Moreover, Saussure argues, the replacement need not be made of the same sort of stuff as the original, or even be the same shape and size. Presumably what matters, then, is the role it plays in the game, and the specification of this requires one to relate it to the other pieces and to the board.

If we call the kind of identity condition relevant in the case of the 8.25 p.m. Geneva–Paris express and the knight 'relational' – to distinguish them from the sorts of condition relevant to the question whether a piece of stuff is the same, which might be called 'material' – then Saussure's view is, of course, that the conditions relevant to the question whether two occurrences of the word 'gentlemen' are the same are relational, not material: 'Each time I say the word *Gentlemen!* I renew its substance; each utterance is a new phonic act and a new psychological act. The bond between the two uses of the same word depends neither on material identity nor on sameness of meaning' (*CLG*, 152, 109).

Though this is plausible enough, it is important to note that the position that Saussure wants to maintain is not simply that the identity conditions are relational. For he maintains that they are relational in a very strong sense, namely that the relations in question are purely differential; by which he means that the conditions in question mention only ways in which the entities in question differ from each other, without characterising them positively in any way – 'in language there are only differences *without positive terms*' (*CLG*, 166, 120). If we call identity conditions of this sort 'purely differential', then it is clear that whilst sets of purely differential conditions must be relational, it is not clear that every set of relational conditions is purely differential. For instance, it is conceivable that the 8.25 p.m. Geneva–Paris express was related to another train because it connected with it at Lyon, and that this was one of its identity conditions. But it is hard to see what could be meant by saying that all we have here is a difference between it and other trains which involves no positive terms. Or, to take a different example, the fact that the knight in chess moves as it does would seem to be a positive fact about it, and one moreover which is not obviously relational at all.

So at this stage we must consider what kinds of relations Saussure thought could hold between linguistic entities, and what it was about them which entails that the identity conditions of linguistics entities are not merely relational, but purely differential.

5.3. Linguistic relations

The key discussion of linguistic relations[5] is hard to follow because of the fact that Saussure often speaks vaguely of linguistic terms, or indeed of words, and hardly ever makes use of his canonical terminology of 'signs', 'signifiers', and 'signifieds'. Inev-

itably, that leaves considerable latitude of interpretation, but it
seems clear that what he wishes to maintain is this:

(i) That there are two generic kinds of relation that signifiers
and signifieds can enter into, syntagmatic and associative

(ii) That the specific kinds of syntagmatic and associative relations which relate signifiers to signifiers are different from
those which relate signifieds to signifieds

(iii) That the identity of a particular signifier or signified is purely
differential

(iv) That a system of signs results from the pairing of a system
of signifiers with one of signifieds; moreover, signs as such
have a value and are not purely differential entities

I shall discuss the first two points in the remainder of this
section and the other two in the next chapter.

5.3.1. Syntagmatic and associative relations

There are, Saussure argues, two different kinds of relation that
linguistic terms can enter into. The first, which he calls 'syntagmatic', is based on the the linear nature of language and holds
between terms which are 'chained together', so that syntagmatic
relations are sequential. One example he gives is that of the
relation between 're-' and 'read' in the syntagm 're-read', so called
because it is a combination of elements which are syntagmatically
related. Saussure says that syntagmatic relations hold between
an item and everything that precedes or follows it, so that we
can presumably say that in 'God is good', which he cites as a
syntagm, 'is' stands in a syntagmatic relation to 'God' and to
'good'. In other words, 'God —— good' is a context in which 'is'
can occur.

Whilst the details of his argument are perhaps not very clear,
it is evident that Saussure thinks that both the importance of
and the need for syntagmatic relations follow from the principle
of the Linearity of the Signifier. Hence the importance which
he attaches to the principle, on which he claims depends the
whole mechanism of language (3.3). So for him it is not simply
a matter of brute fact that syntagmatic relations are important;
this is a fact that follows from a fundamental semiological
principle.

But is the fact that 're-' and 'read' are related syntagmatically
a fact about *langue* or one about *parole*? It would seem that

Saussure must give the first answer; otherwise, he would not be in a position to say in what way *langue* is a system. But, somewhat disconcertingly, he writes as though it is because of the nature of discourse that such relations exist. Such a relation is, he says, '*in praesentia*. It is based on two or more terms that occur in an effective series' (*CLG*, 171, 123). All this suggests that syntagmatic relations are, after all, facts of *parole*.[6] We shall see how Saussure attempted to resolve this tension later; but for the time being it is important to note that unless syntagmatic relations hold between elements of *langue* it is difficult to see that any account can be given in Saussurean terms of the way in which the latter form a system.

The second relation, which Saussure calls 'associative', exists in virtue of similarities of form and meaning which hold between a given item and other items to which it is not syntagmatically related. For example, 'teaching' might be associated with the group of terms {teaching, (to) teach, (we) teach ... }, in which there is something in common between the idea expressed and its signifier in each case; or it might be associated with the series {walking, singing, dancing ... }, because they all contain a verb stem and the signifier '-ing', which signifies the same thing in each case; or it might be associated with the series {training, lecturing, tutoring, educating ... }, in virtue of similarities of meaning; or it might be associated with the series {teasel, teatime, teapoy ... }, simply because of the perceived similarity of the speech sounds realising the initial syllable of the signifier.[7]

Clearly, though these are all relations of the same generic type – that is, they are all associative relations – they are different, depending on the basis of the comparison (cf. (ii) in 5.3). For instance, the second group is structure-dependent and depends on similarities between signifiers and signifieds at a certain point in that structure, whereas the third group is not structure-dependent and concerns only contrasts between signifieds, i.e., ones which describe ways in which a teacher may impart information to a pupil.

Unlike syntagmatic relations, associative ones are 'outside discourse' and 'are not supported by linearity' (*CLG*, 171, 123). Thus there is no difficulty in principle in maintaining that these relations relate elements of *langue* and therefore that 'their seat is in the brain; they are part of the inner storehouse that makes up the language of each speaker. [Moreover] the associative relation unites terms *in absentia* in a potential mnemonic series'

(ibid.). So if there is a worry about associative relations, it is not
because it is hard to see how in principle they relate items belonging to *langue*. The worry is rather one about the vagueness
of the idea of relations that rest simply on the fact that groups
of terms have 'something in common'. Will there not be far too
many such relations? And won't many of those of the fourth
kind delineated – i.e., ones resting on perceived similarities between speech events that realise signifiers, such as that between
'teach' and 'teatime' – invariably be of no linguistic interest?

However, as we shall see, Saussure's implicit answers to the
two main problems mentioned so far (the question whether syntagmatic relations belong to *langue* or *parole* and the worry about
the vagueness of the expression 'associative relation') are connected.

5.3.2. Language, syntagmatic relations, and vagueness

The question whether syntagmatic relations pertain to *langue* or
parole is one which reveals considerable tension in Saussure's
thought. For though he cites a number of sentences as examples
of syntagms ('God is good', 'If the weather is nice we'll go out'
[*CLG*, 170, 123]) and in his lectures argues that the notion of a
syntagm can be applied to sentences as well as to complex words
(Engler 2, 283), he also maintains that it follows from the *langue/
parole* distinction that the sentence is a unit of *parole*.

There are, nevertheless, many more or less explicit hints in
the students' notes of a solution to the problem. There is, to
begin with, a very clear statement: 'This question of the order
of sub-units in the word recalls exactly that of the place of
words in the sentence' (Engler 2, 278B).[8] So Saussure had one
powerful reason for treating the syntagms 're-do' and 'God is
good' in the same way. Either both belong to *langue* or both
to *parole*.

Second, as Saussure goes on to say, syntagmatic and associative
relations are interdependent: '...they mutually condition each
other. In fact, spatial co-ordinations help to create associative
co-ordinations, which are in turn necessary for analysis of the
parts of the syntagm' (*CLG*, 177, 128). For example, consider
the verb 'un-do' (French *dé-faire*). The syntagmatic relations between its parts, can be represented thus:

Moreover, the associative series 'comprising units that have an element in common with the syntagm' can be represented as follows:

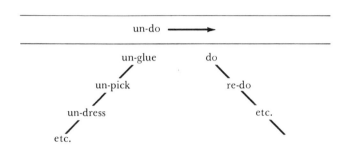

Now, it is clear that the possibility of relating the two representations in this kind of way is not for Saussure a contingent matter:

> To the extent that the other forms float around *défaire* [*un-do*] ... these words can be decomposed into subunits. This is just another way of saying that they are syntagms. *Défaire* [*un-do*] could not be analysed, for instance, if the other forms containing *de-* [*un-*] or *faire* [*do*] disappeared from the language. It would be but a simple unit, and its two parts could not be placed in opposition. (*CLG*, 178, 129)

In other words, a condition of the syntagmatic opposition between 'un-' and 'do' is that each of them belongs to an (a different) associative series. But it is equally true that a condition of each of them belonging to an associative series is that they should stand in syntagmatic opposition to each other.[9]

So it would seem that Saussure must treat both kinds of relation in the same way; either both belong to *langue* or both to *parole*. But since the latter option would leave him with no account at all of the way in which *langue* is systematic, the only tenable one is the first. Moreover, as we saw, sentential syntagms have to be treated in the same way as morphological ones. So the conclusion to which Saussure is deeply committed is that sentential syntagms belong to *langue*.

Why then did he hesitate to draw this conclusion? Part of the difficulty is clearly connected with his attempt to draw a distinction between the concrete and abstract objects of linguistics. Since the categories needed to describe sentential syntagms are abstract, something would have to give at this point. Second, drawing this conclusion might seem to diminish the role allotted to *parole* in Saussure's theory, in that it would leave next to no choice for a speaker, leading us to the conclusion that, to paraphrase Lévi-Strauss, it is language which speaks through men rather than men through language.

Even so, the text of *CLG*, together with its sources, which are more detailed on this point, shows that Saussure did see how to incorporate into his system the conclusion that sentential syntagms belong to *langue*. Doing this calls for a distinction between a type and its exemplification or specimen:

> To language [*langue*] rather than to speaking [*parole*] belong the syntagmatic types that are built upon regular forms.... When a word like *indécorable* arises in speaking ... its appearance supposes a fixed type, and this type is in turn possible only through remembrance of a sufficient number of similar words belonging to language (*impardonable* 'unpardonable', *intolérable* 'intolerable', *infatigable* 'indefatigable', etc.). (*CLG*, 173, 125)

Because of his worries about abstractions, Saussure insists 'that types exist only if language has registered a sufficient number of specimens'. But, subject to this qualification, he is prepared to countenance sentential types; for example, one corresponding to the sentence *Que vous dit-il?* 'What does he say to you?' In this case what one does, he says, is to treat an element within a type as variable:

$$Que \left\{ \begin{array}{l} lui \\ me \\ vous \\ nous \end{array} \right\} dit\text{-}il? \qquad \text{(Engler 2, 294E)}$$

This is typical of the knowledge we possess of what to vary within a unity to make a difference. Moreover, the probable mechanisms involved in speech involve both syntagmatic types and associative groups: 'We speak uniquely by means of syntagms, and the probable mechanism is that we have these *types of syntagms* in the head, *and that at the moment of employing them we bring into play* the associations' (Engler 2, 294B). Thus, if a Frenchman utters *Marchons!* ('Let's walk') it is the oppositions between it and the forms *Marche!* ('Thou walk') and *Marchez!* ('You walk') that affect his choice:

> In reality the idea evokes not a form but a whole latent system that makes possible the oppositions necessary for the formation of the sign. By itself the sign would have no signification. If there were no forms like *marche! marchez!* against *marchons!*, certain oppositions would disappear, and the value of *marchons!* would be changed *ipso facto*. (CLG, 179, 130)

So Saussure's way of dealing with his worry about the abstractness of the descriptions of sentential syntagms is to insist that they are based on specimens, whilst his solution to the problem of choice in *parole* is to allow the speaker freedom to choose between opposed items in a fixed frame.

It has, of course, to be conceded that his notion of types was largely embryonic, and that he gives no more than a sketch of how items on different levels are to be related.[10] Even so, Saussure was clearly in a position to treat sentential syntagms in the same way as he did complex words, and thus treat syntagmatic relations in the same way as he treated associative ones, that is as items belonging to *langue*.

Moreover, the interdependence of syntagmatic and associative relations means that the idea of the latter is not so vague as the original description of it – as a relation holding between linguistic units having something in common – suggests it is. For there is a formal constraint on items related in this way, namely that they must stand in opposition to each other in a context; that is, they must be substitutable for each other in a syntagm. So we can ignore the fourth type of example Saussure cites, the one in which all that two units have in common is a similarity between the speech events which realise their signifiers.

Finally, it should by now be clear why Saussure wants to maintain that the identity conditions for every sign are relational. For apart from its syntagmatic relations, together with the constellation of associative relations that it enters into, the sign 'would have no signification' (CLG, 179, 130). Thus it is only because

Marchons! is opposed to *Marchez!* and *Marche!* that it has the value it has. But the same principle applies equally to more complex syntagms, including sentences:

> To frame the question que *vous* dit il? 'What does he say to *you?*'
> the speaker varies one element of a latent syntactical pattern, e.g.
> que *te* dit il? 'What does he say to *thee?*' que *nous* dit il? 'What does
> he say to *us?*' etc., until his choice is fixed on the pronoun *vous*.
> In this process, which consists of eliminating mentally everything
> that does not help to bring out the desired differentiation at the
> desired point, associative groupings and syntagmatic patterns
> both play a role. (*CLG*, 180, 130)

The principle that linguistic units have no significance apart from their syntagmatic and associative relations, and so necessarily belong to a system, is the central thesis of Saussurean structuralism. For on it depends the determination of what Saussure calls values: 'Whatever might be the order of relations, the word is above all a member of a system. This is important for the determination of value; but even before speaking of value, it is necessary to assert that words appear as terms of a system' (*SM*, 90; Engler 2, 251). But before we turn to Saussure's description of the relation between system and value, we should note that whilst his argument that the identity conditions of linguistic terms are relational seems compelling, it is not clear that they are purely differential. We shall return to this issue later (7.4).

5.4. Summary and prospect

In this chapter we have been concerned with why, in Saussure's view, linguistic items must form a system, and the nature of the relations which hold between the elements of that system. We began by considering why Saussure was so concerned to insist that the entities with which linguistics is concerned are concrete and not abstract. This was not simply a reminder that to consider signifiers and signifieds on their own is to treat them as abstractions, but the expression of a worry that so-called abstract entities, e.g., cases and case endings, are not psychologically real. If they are not, then the kinds of analysis that linguists have done have no foundation in the 'nature of things'. Furthermore,

there is clearly a worry that since linguistic analysis involves seg-
mentation of the phonic chain, there may be indefinitely many
ways of doing this. But in that case which, if any, of the possible
analyses can claim to be the correct one?

Saussure's answer to this question is that it is the one which
correctly reconstructs the underlying system to which the concrete entities belong. But why must linguistic units belong to a
system? The first answer Saussure gives, namely that it is because
many signs, though arbitrary, are only relatively so, rightly draws
attention to the importance of system, even if the way in which
it does so is confused. However, the most that this argument can
establish, it seems, is that the identification of complex signs
involves relating them to a system. So a further argument is
needed to show that the identification of all signs depends on
so relating them.

This argument raises the central question of synchronic identity: In virtue of what can two occurrences of a word be said to
be the same? Saussure's answer to this question, in the course
of evoking a number of forceful analogies with the 8.25 p.m.
Geneva–Paris express and the knight in chess, maintains that
there are two reasons why we count two separate speech events
as instances of the same word, e.g., 'Gentlemen'. First, each of
them differs in the same way from instances of other words in
the language; second, the differences there are between them
are not of any systematic significance. Because this is so, their
identity conditions are not material, but relational. Moreover,
they are relational in a very special sense; namely, they involve
only differences without positive terms, and so are purely
differential.

Clearly, to know in what ways instances of the same word differ
from instances of other words in the language, one must know
in what kinds of linguistically significant ways words and other
linguistic units may be related to each other. There are, Saussure
argues, two such ways. First, they might be related as 're-' and
'do' are related in 're-do'; that is, syntagmatically. Or, second,
they might be related as 'walking' and 'singing' are related, in
virtue of certain similarities of form and meaning; that is, associatively. Indeed, Saussure argues that all linguistic units are
systematically related to other such units by both kinds of
relation.

But do such relations pertain to *langue* or to *parole*? Clearly, only if they pertain to *langue* has Saussure succeeded in principle in giving an account of the way in which *langue* is a system of signs, yet he says that syntagmatic relations pertain to *parole*. However, I have argued that by distinguishing syntagmatic types and their instances he was in principle able to treat both types of relation as ones pertaining to *langue*, and, moreover, that he was therefore in a position to treat sentential syntagms in the same way as morphological ones. Furthermore, he was clearly committed to doing this, even though there were a number of reasons why he hesitated to do it.

Thus the foundations of Saussure's account of the way in which a *langue* is a complex system of entities are now laid. There are, however, two unfinished pieces of business. First, though it is clear why the identity conditions of the elements of such a system are relational, it is not so far clear why they are purely differential. Second, it remains to be seen what is the relation between belonging to such a system and having a special kind of value, namely a pure value. It is to these issues that we now turn.

6

LANGUAGE AS A SYSTEM
OF SIGNS
IV: Values, differences, and reality

We have now reached the climax of Saussure's argument, and the chapter in which it is developed, Part 2, Chapter 4, is arguably the most important in the book. However, not only does the chapter raise a number of very difficult issues, such as the relation of language to thought and reality, but it is also a more than usually complicated compilation of sources, so it is at times far from easy to follow. Moreover, as we shall see, Saussure's argument is not helped by the development of two incompatible metaphors to explain his key term 'value'. The prominence given to these much-quoted metaphors tends to overshadow his central thesis that in a language items which contrast with each other reciprocally define each other's value, even though this is a thesis which arguably stands or falls independently of the validity of the metaphors.

We shall begin by tracing Saussure's introduction of the term 'value' and considering the ways in which it differs from the related terms 'sense' and 'signification'. Next we shall consider Saussure's explanations of why the values in question are pure values, that is ones which arise from the system itself, and are in no way determined extrasystematically. Finally, we shall examine the account given of the connection between values and differences before going on to discuss Saussure's paradox that

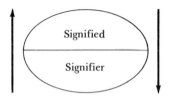

Figure 6.1

'in language there are only differences *without positive terms*.
Whether we take the signified or the signifier, language has
neither ideas nor sounds that existed before the linguistic system,
but only conceptual and phonic differences that have issued
from the system' (*CLG*, 166, 120).

6.1. System and values

Values are first and foremost products of a system for Saussure:
'... *even before speaking of value, it is necessary to state that words
present themselves as terms of a system*' (*SM*, 90). The system in
question is, of course, the set of syntagmatic and associative relations that hold between the concrete entities of a *langue*. But
precisely how does the term 'value' relate to terms already introduced: 'signified', 'concept', and especially 'signification'?

Saussure admits that 'value' appears to be synonymous with
'sense' or 'signification', but nevertheless insists that it is distinct.
Recalling the schematic representation of the sign (fig. 6.1), he
identifies its signification with the counterpart of the signifier,
which is, of course, a signified, adding that to think of a sign or
term in this way is to consider it as an isolated absolute whole.
But this is in his view a partial and misleading view. For the sign
or term can also be seen at the same time as the counterpart of
other signs or terms (fig. 6.2). The terms of which it is the
counterpart are, of course, the other terms of its *langue* to which
it is related syntagmatically or associatively; and it is these relations which determine its value. Hence: 'Language is a system
of interdependent terms in which the value of each term results
solely from the simultaneous presence of the others' (*CLG*, 159,
114). Now, since values are necessarily the product of a system,
the term 'value' would seem to have quite different connotations
from the term 'signification', since the latter as used traditionally
has no necessary connection with a system. So the question arises

Figure 6.2

whether there is any work left for the latter term in Saussure's theory, since if its use arises from adopting a partial point of view it is hard to see how it could be anything other than misleading.

However, to understand Saussure's answer to this question, we must look at the two not obviously compatible metaphors to which he appeals to explain what a value is. According to the first, values are like units of exchange; according to the second, they are the products of the interaction of two otherwise undifferentiated substances, thought and sound.[1]

6.2. Values and exchange

Appealing to an economic model, Saussure argues that, even outside language, values are composed of two elements: '(1) of a *dissimilar* thing that can be *exchanged* for the thing of which the value is to be determined; and (2) of *similar* things that can be *compared* with the things of which the value is to be determined' (*CLG*, 159, 115). For instance, to know the value of a five-franc piece one has to know what one can buy with it, e.g., a loaf of bread, a newspaper, etc., and how it compares with 'a similar value of the same system, e.g. a one-franc piece, or with coins of another system (a dollar, etc.)' (ibid.). Analogously, a word can be exchanged for an idea or compared with other words. However, just as one cannot know the value of a five-franc piece by knowing only what it can be exchanged for – for if that is all one knows, one does not know whether one has paid a lot or a little for one's purchase – one cannot discover the signification of a word only by considering that for which it can be exchanged; one must also relate it to the other words with which it can be compared and with which it contrasts.

Saussure goes on to give a number of examples of the way in which the systematic contrasts between a word and other words determine its value. For instance, the French *mouton* does not mean the same as the English 'sheep', even though both might be used with the same signification. This is so because in English there is another word, 'mutton', which is used when speaking of the cooked animal, whereas in French the same word signifies live animal and cooked meat. In other words, there is a contrast in English between 'sheep' and 'mutton' which does not obtain in French between *mouton* and some other word.[2] This is an illustration of the principle that in a language words which contrast with each other reciprocally define one another's value. Hence the content of a word 'is really fixed only by the concurrence of everything that exists outside of it' (*CLG*, 160, 115).

The principle that values are reciprocally defined by the relations that obtain between terms that contrast with each other applies, Saussure maintains, not only to words but to linguistic terms of all kinds. For instance:

> The value of a French plural does not coincide with that of a Sanskrit plural even though their signification is usually identical; Sanskrit has three numbers instead of two (*my eyes, my ears, my arms, my legs*, etc. are dual); it would be wrong to attribute the same value to the plural in Sanskrit and in French; its value clearly depends on what is outside and around it. (*CLG*, 161, 116)

So in general we can say that the content or value of any linguistic term is fixed by its comparison class, that is the set of terms with which it contrasts.

Amongst the evidence cited by Saussure that this is so is the fact that words do not have exact equivalents in meaning in other languages, which they would do if they stood for pre-existing ideas. Because of this we do not even find the same temporal distinctions made in other languages: 'Hebrew does not recognize even the fundamental distinctions between past, present, and future' (ibid.), whilst the crucial lexicalised distinction made in Slav languages between perfective and imperfective verbs is difficult for a Frenchman to understand, since it is not made in French. Hence, Saussure argues, in all of these cases we are dealing with *values* which arise from the system. Moreover, if these values are taken to correspond to concepts, 'it is understood that the concepts are purely differential and defined not by their positive content, but negatively by their relations with the other terms of the system' (*CLG*, 162, 117). It follows that the schema which 'symbolises signification' cannot be taken as primitive (see fig. 6.1). This is so because the signified is not determinable in isolation from all the other elements of the system, so that the schema is 'only a way of expressing the existence of a certain value circumscribed in the system by its opposition to other terms' (*SM*, 91).

The upshot of this discussion is, therefore, that the term 'signification' should only be used with the clear recognition that it is parasitic on the term 'value'. As such it is clearly dispensable, though in fact Saussure does not dispense with it. Indeed, there are occasions on which he uses it where it does not seem to be parasitic on the term 'value', e.g. in the sentence 'Modern French *mouton* can have the same signification as English *sheep*, but not the same value' (*CLG*, 160, 115). In these cases, though, it is hard to see how it could be a term belonging to *langue*; presumably Saussure's thought is that sometimes when speaking a Frenchman may clearly be speaking about sheep and not mutton, even though the distinction is not marked lexically. But this, if true, is a fact of *parole*.

Saussure's economic metaphor obviously raises the question of what precisely is being exchanged and what compared. At this point it is important to distinguish between a unit of currency and the coins or notes which have the value of the unit but which are not to be identified with it (Harris 1987, 121). Now, since what is exchanged in return for goods are coins, and what belongs to a currency system are its units, then if the analogy is to be exact Saussure should maintain that what is exchanged are tokens of signifiers for signifieds, and that it is signifiers that are compared with other signifiers. But taken in this way the analogy is doubly useless from Saussure's point of view. For, waiving difficulties about the idea that tokens of signifiers are literally exchangeable for signifieds, exchanges would on this account belong to *parole*, since the occurrence of a token of a signifier is a fact of *parole*. Second, it is difficult to see how the content of a signified could be determined only by relations between signifiers, which, according to the analogy, are the entities corresponding to units of currency. That is presumably why Saussure speaks non-canonically of comparisons between words or else between signs. But the latter of these comparisons clearly departs from the analogy, since in a system of currency what is compared are the units, not both the units and what they can be exchanged for.

Another respect in which the analogy is less than ideal from Saussure's point of view is that the goods for which coins can be exchanged can have values other than monetary ones, so that monetary values may in part reflect some other system of values. But he clearly does not want to say anything analogous about signifieds, for to do so would of course undermine the strong version of the principle of the Arbitrariness of the Sign to which he is committed (3.2).

It could, however, be argued that, flawed though the economic metaphor is, Saussure's argument at this point does not depend essentially on it. In particular, it might be said that his claim that in a language items which contrast with each other reciprocally define each other's values is a development of his thesis that linguistic items can be identified only in terms of the syntagmatic and associative relations they stand in to other items of a *langue*, and as such should be assessed on its merits. Moreover, an independent argument, the translation argument, is advanced in support of it. This is plausible; but it will be convenient to defer the question of what remains of Saussure's argument without the appeal to the economic metaphor until we have considered the second of the metaphors adduced to explain the idea of a value (6.4).

6.3. Thought–sound

The second metaphor involves a contrast between form and substance, in which a *langue* is likened to a form which differentiates otherwise amorphous substances. Considered in abstraction from language, ideas are, Saussure argues, amorphous, so that 'nothing is distinct before the appearance of language' (*CLG*, 155, 112). Further, before the appearance of language, sounds do not 'yield predelimited entities' – a conclusion which is hardly surprising in the light of the earlier discussion of the French word *nu* (2.1.1). The linguistic fact therefore has to be pictured[3] 'as a series of contiguous subdivisions marked off on both the indefinite plane of jumbled ideas (A) and the equally vague plane of sounds (B). [Figure 6.3] gives a rough idea of it.' (*CLG*, 156, 112). So the effect of language on thought is not to create a

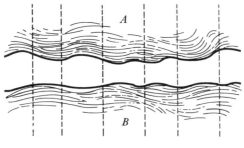

Figure 6.3

phonic means for the expression of pre-existing ideas, as the nomenclaturist would have us believe (3.1). The fact is that it serves

> as a link between thought and sound, under conditions that of necessity bring about the reciprocal delimitation of units. . . . Neither are thoughts given material form nor are sounds transformed into mental entities; the somewhat mysterious fact is rather that 'thought–sound' implies division, and that language works out its units while taking shape between two shapeless masses. (*CLG*, 156, 112)

This somewhat mysterious fact is illustrated by an analogy: A change in the atmospheric pressure of the air in contact with a sheet of water will produce a series of waves, and it is these 'which resemble the coupling of thought with phonic substance' (ibid.). It follows that 'linguistics then works in the borderland where the elements of sound and thought combine; *their combination produces a form, not a substance*' (*CLG*, 157, 113). But not only are the elements combined in thought–sound amorphous considered in themselves, but the choice of 'a given slice of sound to name a given idea is completely arbitrary. If this were not true, the notion of value would be compromised, for it would include an externally imposed element. But actually values remain entirely relative' (ibid.). Indeed, though Saussure does not say this, this last point suggests an argument for both the claim that values are relative and the claim that there are no pre-linguistic ideas. For if the strong version of the principle of the Arbitrariness of the Sign is true, and the identity conditions of

linguistic entities are purely differential (5.3.2), then it is hard
to see how values could be other than relative to a *langue*. Moreover, the existence of pre-linguistic ideas would have to be sus-
pect, since their existence might categorially motivate signs that
express them (3.2).

In this respect the current analogy suits Saussure's overall
position better than the economic metaphor does, since the latter
allows for the existence of independently determinable values.
However, if the strong version of the principle of the Arbitrariness of the Sign should at best be treated as not proven, as we
argued it should, then any argument which, like the present one,
appeals to it should be treated with considerable caution. Moreover, reflection on the diagram and its accompanying explanations
suggests that in most respects the current analogy is much more
obscure than the economic metaphor. For the claim that a language is a form which differentiates otherwise shapeless masses
strongly suggests that signifiers are slices of sound. But this is
difficult to reconcile with Saussure's claim that they are in fact
acoustic images, i.e., representations of sounds (3.1.1). Indeed,
he says explicitly that 'it is impossible for a sound alone, a material
element, to belong to language (*langue*)' (*CLG*, 164, 118). Furthermore, the illustration of how two amorphous masses can
combine to produce a form is not very helpful. For the waves
are produced in the water by the action of the air pressure; but
surely thought, on Saussure's account, has no analogous role to
play in relation to sound. In short, the analogy throws no light
on the way in which the combination of the two masses, thought
and sound, could produce a form, for on Saussure's account no
agent or agency is involved.

Given his general theory, the only possible agents could be
individuals whose speech acts sustain or modify states of their
language without, of course, in his view, intending to do so either
individually or collectively. In other words, the appeal at this
point has to be to the comparison of a language with a game of
chess – bearing in mind, of course, the one fundamental disanalogy that whereas in the latter case players intend to bring
about the states that their moves produce, speakers do not intend
to bring about the changes in their language which result from
their speech acts (4.2). Hence speakers play a role in changing,
and indeed sustaining, their language without intending to do
so. Thus modified, the chess analogy provides a model of the

way in which values depend on language states, and in turn of the way in which these are the product of individual actions, though not ones designed to bring states about. That is presumably why, in the course of discussing the thought–sound metaphor, Saussure hastens to add that the fact that the sign is arbitrary also explains why language has to be viewed as a social fact: 'The arbitrary nature of the sign explains why the social fact alone can create a linguistic system. The community is necessary if values that owe their existence solely to usage and general acceptance are to be set up' (CLG, 157, 113).[4] So the metaphor of thought–sound as both the product of the interaction of two shapeless masses and a form which creates units within them simply does not stand on its own feet. Without the implicit appeal to the chess metaphor, no account of how the two masses are shaped, modified, and changed is available.

6.3.1. Divisions within a continuum

Even so, it might be argued that Saussure is making an important point which is independent of the fruitfulness of his metaphor. That is that different languages do provide systematic but different ways of differentiating things which are not as a matter of brute fact differentiated, or, at least, make different and incongruent distinctions within what is intuitively the same domain. A striking example of this phenomenon, often adduced, is colour terms. In the colour spectrum there are no sharp discontinuities. Moreover, it is *prima facie* difficult to see how colours could be natural similarity classes, since, for instance, a shade of red close to the borderline between red and orange will be more similar to some shades of orange than it is to some shades of red. So the drawing of a boundary between adjacent colours seems to be an arbitrary matter. It should, therefore, not be surprising that

it is an established fact that the colour-terms of particular languages cannot always be brought into one-to-one correspondence with one another: for example, the English word *brown* has no equivalent in French (it would be translated as *brun*, *marron*, or even *jaune*, according to the particular shade and the kind of noun it qualifies); the Hindi word *pīlā* is translated into English as *yellow*, *orange*, or even *brown* (although there are different words for other shades of 'brown'); there is no equivalent to *blue* in Russian – the words *goluboy* and *sinij* (usually translated as 'light blue' and 'dark blue' respectively) refer to what are in Russian distinct colours, not to different shades of the same colour, as their translation into English might suggest. (Lyons 1968, 56)

These, of course, are only a few examples, but it could be argued that there are many more; 'adolescent', for instance, belongs to a system of classification of the ages of man different from that rehearsed by Jacques in *As You Like It*; and according to a famous study there was a major change in the structure of the conceptual field of knowledge and understanding in Middle High German.[5] This study was the work of Trier, who made a distinction between lexical and conceptual fields, the role of the former being to divide the latter into parts. According to Lehrer,

he found, for example, that around 1200, part of the intellectual field consisted of three terms that patterned in the following way:

Wîsheit	
Kunst	*List*

Kunst referred approximately to courtly knowledge, including social behavior, *List* was used for more technical skills or knowledge, and *Wîsheit* was a more general term covering the whole field. By 1300 the intellectual field had changed. *Wîsheit* came to be used in a religious or mystical sense, and *Kunst* was used for more mundane skill and knowledge, having lost its connotation of courtly and social knowledge. *Wissen*, a new term in the intellectual sphere, was used for art, and *List* moved out of the semantic field. (Trier 1931, 1934)

Wîsheit	*Kunst*	*Wissen*

ca. 1300

(Lehrer 1974, 15)

But though these examples do provide important evidence that vocabularies are structured in systematic ways, it is not clear that the underlying idea which unifies them, that of a continuum which is divisible in different ways, is either one that Saussure had in mind or one that is completely generalisable. To begin with, Saussure's comparison of pre-linguistic thought to a 'vague uncharted nebula', though speculative, does not suggest that the world itself is a vague uncharted nebula, or that it consists of continua. Nor does it seem sensible to think of the vague uncharted nebula of pre-linguistic thought as something which itself gets divided up, since, for instance, it is not clear what boundaries it has. The kinds of examples we have been discussing have been concerned with relatively limited domains: colour, ages of man, and kinds of knowledge. Although the isolation of these domains of course requires considerable sophistication, it is essential that they be delimited for purposes of the analysis.[6] But what are the boundaries of thought itself? On Saussure's initial account, thought is more like a cloud or a gas than like a field; i.e., it has no determinate boundaries. Moreover, we must distinguish the kind of precision that arises in our thought from making distinctions within or about its objects from the kind that arises when we make distinctions within or about thought itself.[7]

Second, since the colour spectrum is hardly an object of everyday experience, the literal applicability of arguments which depend on there being different ways of dividing it up is doubtful. It is surely conceivable that people have lived in an environment in which there are no instances of certain parts of the spectrum. Moreover, the work of Berlin and Kay strongly suggests that the differences among colour vocabularies are by no means completely arbitrary (Berlin & Kay 1970). Though it is true that speakers from different languages do not agree about the boundaries between such adjacent colours as green and yellow, speakers of the same language do not always agree about them either. However, considerable uniformity is to be found if we concentrate on the focal points for each colour – that is, the most typical or paradigmatic examples of it – rather than on its boundaries. On the basis of a study of twenty languages supplemented by additional data, Berlin and Kay argued that there is a hierarchy in the importance of colours:

> They find that all languages have terms for black and white. If there is a third term, it will be red. If a language has four terms,

the fourth will be either yellow or green. Languages with five
terms have both yellow and green. A word for blue is the sixth
to emerge, and a term for brown is the seventh. If a language
has eight or more colour words, it will have words for purple,
pink, orange, gray, or some combination. (Lehrer 1974, 153)

It is, moreover, suggested that the order in which colour terms
were added to languages corresponds to the hierarchy, as does
the order in which children learn them. The details of the hy-
pothesis have been questioned,[8] but at the very least it draws
attention to the ways in which apparent diversities may at a
deeper level of explanation exhibit considerable uniformity.
Moreover, given the salience of differences in luminosity and
their importance perceptually, it is perhaps not surprising that
the difference between black and white should have been uni-
versally lexicalised, whilst the very widespread lexicalisation of
the difference between red and green might be explained by
the fact that it has a neurophysiological basis (Lyons 1977, 248).

Third, if the literal applicability of arguments which depend
on there being an arbitrarily divisible continuum is at best highly
questionable in the case of colour, there are many other areas
of experience in which it is hard to see how it could apply at all.
It is surely only in a metaphorical sense that we can in many
domains be said to be presented with a continuum at all; for
example, of extents of water, of masses of trees. And even then
the principles of classification involved in our vocabulary seem
to be far too complex for it to be possible to account for them
on the model in question. Consider for instance terms in English
for extents of water: 'brook', 'bay', 'cove', 'estuary', 'lake', 'ocean',
'pond', 'pool', 'puddle', 'reservoir', 'river', 'sea', 'stream', 'tribu-
tary'. The difference among 'river', 'stream', and 'brook' is one
of size, as is that between 'sea' and 'ocean'. However, the difference between 'sea' and 'lake' is not one of size, but of the nature
of the water (salt/fresh), for a sea, like a lake, can be land-locked
(Sea of Galilee). The difference between 'lake' and 'reservoir' is
one of the intended use of the water. Complex though this system is, it does not mark all distinctions which other languages
think worth marking – for example, that between a river which
empties into the sea and one which does not (fleuve/rivière) – and
no doubt it marks distinctions which other languages do not.
The idea that these are distinctions within a single continuum

which is in some sense neutral between languages just does not seem fruitful.

However, Saussure's claim that a signified is to be defined relationally in terms of the associative and syntagmatic relations in which it stands to other signifieds has no difficulty in principle in accounting for the kind of complexity that I have been discussing, since there seems to be no reason why there should not be a great variety of ways in which a given signified can differ from other signifieds with which it contrasts in virtue of standing in an associative or syntagmatic relation to it. Moreover, not only does Saussure claim that it is because signifieds have to be defined relationally that linguistic terms which contrast with each other reciprocally define each other's values, but also, as we saw, the claim is independent of the economic metaphor as a plausible development in its own right of the thesis that a linguistic item can be identified only in terms of the syntagmatic and associative relations that it has to other items within a *langue* (6.2). So, since Saussure's metaphors have only muddied the waters and there seems to be a way of developing his argument independently of them, it is time to turn our back on them and consider this independent argument.

6.4. Differences, oppositions, and pure values

We saw that Saussure argued that the identity conditions of a linguistic item are relational (5.2) and that the relevant relations are syntagmatic and associative ones which hold between it and other items of a similar kind in a *langue*. Now, it would seem that the link envisaged between possessing a value and belonging to a *langue* is as follows:

(T) The value of a linguistic item is determined by the set of syntagmatic and associative relations that it enters into with other items in a *langue*.

If that is so, then it is clear both why Saussure is so insistent that the values of an item arise from a system and why what he himself says about values is itself so dependent on his claims about the identity conditions of linguistic items.

At this point two closely connected questions arise. First, precisely what kinds of things can have a value, and how many

different kinds of value are there? Second, why did Saussure
think that values are purely negative, involving only differences
without any positive terms?

6.4.1. Kinds of value

The answer to the first question might seem obvious, given the
way in which the term 'value' was introduced as cognate to the
terms 'sense' and 'signification'; namely, that it is signifiers that
have a value. Moreover, the value of a given signifier is its signified, and this we saw has to be defined negatively in terms of
its 'relations with the other terms of the system' (*CLG*, 162, 117).
However, if what makes something a value is the fact that it has
to be so defined, then it is important to note that Saussure maintains that *signifiers* as well as signifieds have to be defined in this
kind of way:

> The conceptual side of value is made up solely of relations and
> differences with respect to the other terms of the language, and
> the same can be said of its material side. The important thing in
> the word is not the sound alone but the phonic differences that
> make it possible to distinguish this word from all others, for dif-
> ferences carry signification. (*CLG*, 163, 117)

Indeed, this follows, he claims, from the principle of the Arbitrariness of the Sign. Since the relation between a signifier and
its signified is radically arbitrary, no signifier is any more appropriate than any other to express a given signified, so that it
can never 'be based on anything except its non-coincidence with
the rest. *Arbitrary* and *differential* are two correlative qualities'
(ibid.).

But if signifiers have to be defined differentially, and according to (T) being so defined makes something a value, then ought
not signifiers to count as values as much as signifieds? An initial
response to this question is no doubt that surely signifiers have
values but are not themselves values. But in that case (T) is
insufficient to explain why signifieds are values, for, as we have
just seen, signifiers too have to be identified negatively in terms
of their relations with other terms of the system. Indeed, according to Saussure, not only do signifiers as well as signifieds
have to be so defined, but so do phonemes.[9] These are, he says,

'above all else opposing, relative, and negative entities' (*CLG*, 164, 119). This is so presumably because we can say that the phoneme /p/ occurs initially in the English word /pat/ only because it there contrasts functionally with /b/, /c/, /f/, etc. The contrast is functional in the sense that substitution of one of the other phonemes for it would produce a token of another word, for instance /bat/, /cat/, /fat/, etc. Similarly, /a/ is functional in /pat/ because it contrasts there with /e/, /i/, etc. But there are languages in which the contrast utilised in English between /p/ and /b/ is not significant, so that in these 'a *p-sound* and a *b-sound* . . . are in free variation, in the sense that the substitution of the one for the other in the same phonetic environment preserves the type–token identity of the resulting forms' (Lyons 1977, 233).

In other words, whether a sound is functionally significant in a language depends on what contrasts and oppositions are counted as significant by the phonological system of the language. It is this point that Saussure is making when he writes that 'I can even pronounce the French *r* like German *ch* in *Bach*, *doch*, etc., but in German I could not use *r* instead of *ch*, for German gives recognition to both elements and must keep them apart' (*CLG*, 165, 119). Thus we must conclude that signifiers and signifieds are both values, but ones of different kinds, because the kinds of syntagmatic and associative relations that hold between the former are different from those that hold between the latter. Moreover, it is important to note that as well as being a value, a signifier can be said to *have* a value, namely the signified with which it is conventionally correlated.

So we must distinguish two claims:

  (i) A linguistic entity *is* a value if it is constituted by the set of syntagmatic and associative relations in which it stands to other entities of the same kind, and
 (ii) A linguistic entity *has* a value if it is correlated with a signified

But what then does it mean to say that values are purely negative?

6.4.2. Purely negative values

One thing that could be meant can be illustrated by reference to phonemes, the important point being that for a phoneme to play its role it is necessary and sufficient that it be distinct from the other phonemes in the system. As Jakobson says, ' . . . it would be perfectly correct for us to say that taken in isolation the [French] nasal *a* phoneme is nothing, because its sole value in French is its non-identity with all the other phonemes of the French language' (1978, 64). In other words, the French nasal *a* phoneme is simply different from all the other phonemes of the language, and lacks any positive content of its own, since there is no answer to the question 'What does the French nasal *a* phoneme signify?'

So presumably what Saussure meant by calling phonemes negative entities was that they lack any positive content, and that to play their linguistic role all they need is to be different from the other phonemes in the same system. Hence he would have agreed with Jakobson's claim:

> The linguistic value of the nasal *a* phoneme in French, and in general of any phoneme in any language whatever, *is only its power to distinguish the word containing this phoneme from any words which, similar in all other respects, contain some other phoneme.* Thus *sang* is distinguished from *son, sein, ça, sceau, sou, si, su,* etc. (1978, 61)

Thus we can say that though phonemes *are* values, since they are determined by the reciprocal oppositions in which they stand to other phonemes, they do not *have* values, since they signify nothing.

But, as Jakobson urges, the characteristic of phonemes of being purely negative, of lacking content, as well as of being relative and opposing entities, is not a characteristic of other linguistic entities, as Saussure claims. For instance, Saussure argues that letters are, like phonemes, purely negative and differential:

> (1) The signs used in writing are arbitrary; there is no connection, for example, between the letter *t* and the sound that it designates.
> (2) The value of letters is purely negative and differential. The same person can write *t,* for instance, in different ways:

> The only requirement is that the sign for *t* not be confused in his script with the signs used for *l, d,* etc.

(3) Values in writing function only through reciprocal opposition within a fixed system that consists of a number of letters. This third characteristic, though not identical to the second, is closely related to it, for both depend on the first. (*CLG*, 165, 119)

Revealingly, Saussure argues that being purely negative and differential, the second characteristic, is closely related to the third, the existence of reciprocal oppositions within a fixed system. However, not only does he not tell us what the nature of this relationship is, but in the case in question the third characteristic is present but the second is not. For the letter *t* not only *is* a value, but it also *has* one, namely the phoneme /t/ which it designates. As Jakobson says,

> It goes without saying that the existence of a determinate system of graphemes is a necessary prerequisite for the arrangement of each letter. But the thing which is of primary significance here is the specific, positive value of each grapheme. Of course the letter *beta* must be distinguished from the letters *alpha*, *gamma*, *delta*, etc., but the *raison d'être* for the Greek grapheme *beta* is its designation of the phoneme *b*, and all other graphemes have a similar task to perform. The graphic image functions as a signifier and the phoneme as its signified. (1978, 65)

The crucial point is this: The characteristic of being purely negative and differential is not entailed by that of being constituted by a set of reciprocal oppositions within a system. Thus what is true of phonemes, namely that they have no positive content and have a merely differentiating role, is not necessarily true of signifiers and signifieds.

However, it might be urged that as a criticism of Saussure this misses the point. For the positive content that a grapheme or signifier has on this account arises only from the correlation that exists between it and a signified. But the result of that correlation, a sign, does not have a purely differential role. Moreover, this is something Saussure would admit, for he claims that

> although both the signified and the signifier are purely differential and negative when considered separately, their combination is a positive fact; it is even the sole type of facts that language has, for maintaining the parallelism between the two classes of

differences is the distinctive function of the linguistic institution. (*CLG*, 166, 120)[10]

In other words, though it is not true that the only role that signifiers have is a differential one (because of the correlations that exist between them and signifieds), the fact remains that, this correlation apart, they are constituted only by reciprocal oppositions within a system. Hence, if we consider them only from this point of view, they are purely negative and differential entities, as indeed are signifieds. It is to the consideration of this claim that we now turn.

6.4.3. Differences

Because of its intrinsic interest and philosophical implications, we shall restrict our discussion to the case of signifieds. The claim that signifieds are purely negative and differential entities has arguably two different sources in Saussure's thought. One source, connected with the metaphor of the amorphous pre-linguistic masses of thought and sound, argues that the negative and differential role of signifieds arises from the fact that they occupy, or correspond to, an arbitrarily chosen part of a contin-uum which has no positive features to distinguish it essentially from other arbitrarily chosen parts. Culler, for instance, sees this as an important source of Saussure's ideas:

> We began by noting that there is no natural link between signifier and signified, and then, trying to explain the arbitrary nature of the linguistic sign, we saw that both signifier and signified were arbitrary divisions or delimitations of a continuum (a sound spec-trum on the one hand and a conceptual field on the other). (1976, 29)

However, we have seen that there are many reasons to doubt the literal applicability of the idea that for every domain there is a continuum which is arbitrarily divided by the terms belonging to that domain (6.3.1). Moreover, there is something quite un-Saussurean about the idea of the existence of language-independent continua; that is, continua which are given, so that their existence is independent of that of any particular language.[11]

A second source of Saussure's view that signifieds are purely negative and differential entities rests on the thesis that signifieds which contrast reciprocally define each other's value. Hence, the value of a given signified is not given or language-independent. What it is is determined by the language-specific relations in which it stands to other items in the same language. Apart from the fact that, unlike the first source, it does not presuppose the existence of language-independent continua in each domain, this argument has a further advantage. For the relations in question could be very various and not just those required to partition a given conceptual space or field.

Now, terms that differ from each other must contrast in some way; A and B cannot just be different without being different in some respect. However, the existence of a difference between two terms does not always give rise intuitively to an opposition. The signified 'chair', for instance, differs from the signified 'three', since the former but not the latter contains the component (For sitting on), but intuitively they are not opposed terms. In other words, difference is not sufficient for opposition.

However, if two signifieds belong to what is intuitively the same domain, then difference does seem to give rise to opposition in the sense that 'X is an A' implies 'X is not a B', and vice versa: 'X is a B' implies 'X is not an A'. For instance, 'X is a male' implies 'X is not a female', and vice versa; 'X is hot' implies 'X is not cold' and vice versa; and 'X is Tuesday' implies 'X is not Sunday' and vice versa.[12] In the first two of these cases the contrast is binary, but not in the third; for whilst male and female exhaust the domain of gender, Tuesday and Sunday do not exhaust that of days of the week. There is, moreover, a difference, pointed out by Lyons, between the first two cases of binary opposition. For whereas 'X is not male' implies 'X is female', and vice versa, 'X is not hot' does not imply 'X is cold' any more than 'X is not cold' implies 'X is hot'. This is no doubt connected to the fact that the signifieds 'hot' and 'cold' stand at the end point of a scale, in between which another pair of opposites, 'warm'/ 'cool', is interposed (Lehrer 1974, 26). Furthermore, 'hot' and 'cold' are used to grade, so that '*This soup is hot* implies that it is hot relative to a certain implicit norm, either soup or perhaps liquids served at a meal or even liquids in general. The norm is different, however, in sentences like *Paris is hot in the summer'* (ibid.). Following Lyons, we shall call gradable opposites like

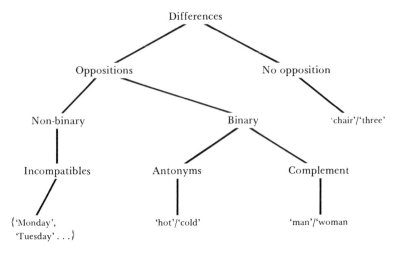

Figure 6.4

'hot'/'cold' antonyms, and reserve the term 'complementary' for non-gradable binary opposites such as 'male'/'female' which mutually exhaust some dimension of contrast, in this case gender. Non-binary oppositions such as those involved in the set {'Monday', 'Tuesday', ... , 'Sunday'} we shall call 'incompatible' (Lyons 1977, ch. 9). Thus we have the distinctions shown in Figure 6.4.'[3]

It is an important point that, though there would be no oppositions without differences, not all differences give rise to oppositions. Moreover, it is presumably only those differences which do that are relevant to a signified's definition. In other words, the set of signifieds the relations between which reciprocally define each other are not sets of signifieds which are simply different, but ones which are opposed. This is important, because since a given signified is different from every other signified in indefinitely many respects, it is difficult to see how it would be graspable if its characterisation depended only on differences. We should be adrift in a sea of differences without any principle of relevance. Moreover, oppositions, though they involve differences, also involve similarities. For instance, 'man' and 'woman' are opposed, since the latter contains the component (Female) and the former does not. But for them to be opposed in this way, both *must* contain the component (Animate), and there is no reason why they should not share all their other components, e.g., (Human), (Adult). As Lyons points out,

> we can say that X is married and Y is single, but in all other respects similar. Moreover, we cannot predicate the word 'married' and 'single' of X and Y, unless a certain number of other words are predicable of X and Y. This holds for most, if not all, lexical opposites. Oppositions are drawn along some dimension of similarity. (1977, 286)

Presumably that is why only those differences which give rise to oppositions are relevant to the determination of a signified's content; for it is only if they do so give rise that the content of the one can be said to be delimited by the other. But to reiterate, this can only happen if they have something in common.

So far it is not difficult to see what Saussure might have had in mind when he described signifieds as opposing and relative. It is harder to see what he meant when he described them as negative, claiming that 'in language there are only *differences without positive terms*' (*CLG*, 166, 120). For, as we have seen, not all differences are relevant to the determination of the content of a signified; only those which give rise to oppositions are. Moreover, the latter involve differences within some dimension of similarity.

However, the binary thesis explains what might be meant by saying that an aspect of a signified's content is not positively characterisable. According to this thesis, a signified's content is determined by a series of binary contrasts in which one term is marked and the other unmarked; that is,[14] 'as /b/ may be said to contain the phonological feature of voice, which /p/ lacks, so (it might be said that) "man" and "boy" contain the sense component MALE, which "woman" and "girl" lack' (Lyons 1977, 322). But obviously, whilst this explains what it means for a term to be negatively characterised, it does so in a way which makes it impossible for every term to be so characterised. For one member of a binary opposition must be positively characterised for us to be in a position to say that the other simply lacks a feature that the first possesses. Moreover, there are some well-known difficulties with this proposal. There are two different ways in which a term can fail to contain the component (Male). In the first of these, the lack implies the possession of some other characteristic, i.e., (Female), so that instead of saying that 'woman' lacks the component (Male) we might just as well have said that 'man' lacks the component (Female). But in the second type of case, the lack of (Male) implies nothing about the possession of any other characteristic – from the fact that 'chair' does not contain (Male) we cannot infer anything about what it does contain. Commenting on the notation which uses '(+Male)' to denote possession of the feature (Male), Lehrer writes:

> The advantage of this notation is that it makes explicit the fact that both features, e.g., [+Animate] and [–Animate] belong to the same system. Unfortunately, the use of the – is inconsistent. Sometimes it means that a feature is nonapplicable, and sometimes it specifies a positive feature that contrasts with +, such as characterising [Child] as [–Parent]. If it is clear what positive feature is meant when – is used in this way, there is probably no harm in using this notation. (1974, 60)

Presumably, since it is clear what positive feature is attributed in claiming that 'cow' has (–Male) as a component, there may be no objection to the use of the notation in this case. But 'bullock' creates a problem, since to say that it lacks the component (Male) is not to imply anything about its positive features. These problems apart, the treatment of gradable antonyms in a similar way is, as Lehrer points out, extremely implausible. Apart from the fact that it is not always plausible to characterise 'cold' as (–Hot), part of the source of the difficulty is that they are opposed as end points of a scale and so have to be related not only to each other but to other terms in the scale.

It is of course true that there is no general rule that says which of a dichotomous pair of features is dominant in a given case; in the pair 'stallion'/'horse' it is (+Male), in the pair 'lion'/'lioness' it is (+Female), whilst in the pair 'duke'/'duchess' neither would seem to be. But whilst this might be taken to show that in the language no feature is naturally dominant, it hardly shows that particular signifieds cannot be positively characterised. Apart from the ways I have already discussed in which this can arise, there would seem to be a number of other such ways. For example, a pig is an animal, a buttercup is a flower, etc., so that one important part of the characterisation of the signifieds 'pig' and 'buttercup' is a specification of what kind or sort of thing pigs and buttercups are. But it is hard to see how this could be done purely negatively; e.g., 'To be a buttercup is not to be any one of the following: a rose, a peony, a delphinium, etc., etc.' For apart from the fact that the idea of a closed list of kinds of flowers is highly questionable, to be a buttercup is not just not to be identical with any of the flowers mentioned in the list, for a dog is that, but to be a *flower* that is not any of the other kinds mentioned.

Another type of relation which would seem to need to be positively characterised is that of a part to the whole. One could, for instance, hardly understand what a collar is unless one understood how it related to other parts of a shirt.

> Even more convincing are sets of words like 'second', 'minute', 'hour', 'day', 'week', etc. The meaning of 'day', 'month' and 'year' (and perhaps 'week') could be explained at least partly, without mentioning any part–whole relationships that hold within the set. … But it is in principle impossible to explain the meaning of 'second', 'minute' and 'hour' without specifying the part–whole relationships holding within the set. (Lyons 1977, 314)

Thus a negative definition of the form 'A second is not a minute, and not an hour and not a day …' is not possible, because we cannot say what a minute is without specifying its relation to a second.

So if Saussure's claim that signifieds are purely negative entities is true, we have completely failed to capture any sense in which it is. Indeed, I have argued that only differences which give rise to oppositions are relevant to the determination of a signified's content, and that oppositions presuppose similarities. Moreover, it seems that some of the ways in which signifieds call for positive characterisation do not in any natural sense involve oppositions. For instance, something can be both a buttercup and a flower, so the signifieds 'buttercup' and 'flower' certainly are not opposed to each other. And though, of course, an hour is not a second, it contains seconds.

Thus, not only have we failed to make sense of the claim that signifieds are purely negative and differential entities, but there is good reason to think that there is no way of so doing. But if that is correct, is Saussure's system not then in ruins?

To answer this question it is necessary to distinguish the prin-

ciple (T), that in a language items which contrast with each other
reciprocally define each other's value, from the principle (T1),
that in a language there are only differences without positive
terms. We saw in our discussion of what Saussure has to say
about graphemes that he himself sees the two principles as being
closely connected (6.4.2). However, in at least one way of interpreting the phrase 'purely negative' there is no logical connection
between the two characteristics involved. So there is a strong
prima facie case for arguing that the truth of (T) stands or falls
quite independently of that of the much more dubious (T1).
This is an important result, for the theory of structural linguistics
is strongly committed to (T); hence Lyons's claim that the 'defining characteristic of modern "structural" linguistics is as follows: linguistic units have no validity independently of their
paradigmatic [=associative] and syntagmatic relations with other
units' (1968, 75). But it is not similarly committed to (T1); indeed, the way in which structuralist semantics has developed has
provided the basis for a reasoned critique of the principle. On
the other hand, structuralist and post-structuralist philosophers
often cite (T1) as one of Saussure's major insights. In so doing
they have tried to build on one of the most opaque parts of
Saussure's theory, and one, moreover, which the actual practice
of structural linguistics does not presuppose. So the success of
that practice cannot, if I am right, be used as an argument for
the claim that in language there are no positive terms.

6.5. Summary

In this chapter we have been tracing the ways in which the
threads of Saussure's complex argument come together. In particular we have been concerned first with the connection he
makes between the notion of value and that of system, and second with his claim that values are relative, opposing, and negative
entities, so that in languages there are only differences without
positive terms.

   Since values are products of a system, it is important to note
that the theoretical implications of the term are radically different from that of the term 'signification' which it supplants, since
they are holistic (3.1.1); we cannot first identify a value and then
describe the system to which it belongs, since '*words present themselves as terms of a system*' (*SM*, 90). To illustrate the way in which

values depend on a system, Saussure appeals to two metaphors. In the economic metaphor he argues that, outside of language, values have two features (6.2). There are dissimilar things for which they can be *exchanged*, and similar things with which they can be *compared*. For instance, a five-franc piece can be exchanged for a loaf of bread and compared with a one-franc piece, a ten-franc piece, etc. Analogously, a word can be exchanged for an idea or compared with another word. And just as one can grasp the value of a coin only if one knows what it can be exchanged for and how it is related to other coins of different denominations, so one can grasp the value of a term only if one knows both what it signifies and the relations that obtain between it and terms to which it contrasts.

However, there are a number of respects in which the comparison breaks down. Apart from the obscurity of the notion that words can be exchanged for ideas, the analogy says that what would have to be exchanged are tokens of signifiers, so that the transactions would belong to *parole* and not *langue*. On the other hand, comparisons would have to be between entities corresponding to units of currency, which are signifiers, and not their tokens; but it is difficult to see how such comparisons could account for the values that signifiers *have*, that is the signifieds with which they are associated.

In addition, the analogy has a very serious flaw from Saussure's point of view. The goods for which coins are exchanged have values other than monetary ones which, at least in part, determine their monetary values, so that it is difficult to see how the latter could be a product of the system of currency alone. But if they are not, then they cannot be pure values, and as such radically arbitrary.

In this respect the second of Saussure's metaphors, that of the interaction of two amorphous masses, wind and water, is much better from his point of view (6.3). For the system of differences arising from their interaction, the waves, has no existence independently of it. But there are other difficulties with this comparison. The diagram illustrating the analogy suggests that signifiers should be construed as slices of sound – contrary, of course, to Saussure's view that they are acoustic images (3.1.1). And whilst the waves are a product of the action of the air on the water, Saussure does not wish to allot an analogous role to the thought mass. If language is a form (2.2), then we need some account of the way in which 'something' which is neither thought nor sound provides a principle for structuring both. And if at this point to provide such an account we need to appeal to the chess analogy, as I suggested, then the thought–sound metaphor simply does not stand on its own feet.

As for the argument that, even so, the metaphor does draw attention to an important truth – that languages provide principles for making distinctions within phenomena which present themselves as undifferentiated continua, e.g., the colour spectrum – I argued that it too is wanting (6.3.1). Apart from the fact that the colour spectrum itself is hardly an object of everyday experience, casting doubt on the literal applicability of arguments that something which presents itself as undifferentiated is then differentiated, the work of Berlin and Kay strongly suggests that colour vocabularies are by no means completely arbitrary. So, since Saussure's influential metaphors shed so little light, I tried to describe the way in which his argument develops independently of them, by tracing the relation between a value and a system and the reasons for thinking that values are opposing, relative, and negative entities (6.4).

The connection between a value and the system to which it belongs is, I argued, governed by the principle (T) that the value of a linguistic item is determined by the set of syntagmatic and associative relations that it enters into with other items in a *langue*. Moreover, for Saussure not only are signifieds values, but so are signifiers and phonemes (in the modern sense of that term), though they are, of course, values of different kinds.

However, though signifiers, signifieds, and phonemes all are values, the latter certainly do not *have* a value, since they are not correlated with signifieds (6.4.1). Further, the distinction between being a value and having one is important for the evaluation of the claim that values are purely negative. One thing that Saussure might have meant by this can be illustrated by reference to phonemes. The important point is that for a given phoneme to play its linguistic role – which, in Jakobson's words, is '*to distinguish the word containing this phoneme from any words which, similar in all other respects, contain some other phoneme*' (1978, 62) – it is necessary only that it be different from the other phonemes in the language. It is not also necessary that it have a positive content, i.e., that it should signify something. But if this is what Saussure meant, it is true neither of letters nor of signifiers generally. They do not have a purely differentiating role, for as well as being values they *have* values. Significantly, we noticed that when talking about letters Saussure maintained that the character of being purely negative is closely associated with that of being relative and opposing, even though letters have the latter characteristic but not the former, so that the association cannot be logical. Clearly, phonemes cannot be taken as a model of signifiers.

Finally, we considered the objection that Saussure could hardly have denied that signifiers have values; after all, a *langue* is a system for the correlation of signifiers and signifieds. That granted, the objection continues, he maintains that, this correlation apart, they are constituted only by reciprocal oppositions within a system, so that if we consider them from this point of view alone, they are indeed purely differential and negative, as are signifieds.

However, we did not succeed in making sense of this claim in the case of signifieds (6.4.3). Differences as such do not give rise to oppositions; it is only in those cases in which signifieds (or what they denote) belong to what is intuitively the same domain that they do. Furthermore, though oppositions involve differences, they standardly involve similarities; as Lyons says, 'oppositions are drawn along some dimension of similarity' (1977, 286). But why should the specification of the similarity not count as a positive feature?

The binary thesis suggested an explanation of what it is for a term to be negatively characterised – it is the unmarked term in a binary opposition. But clearly this explanation requires other terms to be positively characterised, other difficulties with the proposal apart. Further, I argued that there are a number of other important semantic relationships which call for a positive characterisation, e.g., kind membership and part–whole relationships.

Thus not only did we fail to make sense of the thesis that signifieds are purely differential and negative entities, but there is good reason to think that this cannot be done. However, it does not follow that Saussure's overall project shipwrecks. For whilst the theory and practice of structural linguistics appeals to the principle (T), it does not appeal to the principle (T1), that in language there are only differences without positive terms. Moreover, (T) does not imply (T1).

7

SUCCESSES AND FAILURES

The preceding chapters have shown something of the scope and ambition of Saussure's project. However incomplete it may have been, it initiated a radically new perspective in the study of language, a veritable Copernican revolution. This insisted that the primary study of a language is a synchronic study of it as a system, in which the main aim is to identify the units of the system and the relations among them. Such units are not mere abstractions, but concrete entities which are psychologically real (5.1), so that there is in principle a determinate system to be reconstructed. Moreover, their value is determined by the relations and oppositions that obtain between them and other items of the system rather than by their history or by other extraneous factors. Of course, if this is the primary study, then it is essential that we should be clear about what belongs to the system and what not; hence the importance of the distinctions between *langue* and *parole* and between synchrony and diachrony. And since the system has to be described by describing the relations among its elements, which are not identifiable independently of it, the importance of Saussure's account of associative and syntagmatic relations is also clear.

We saw that Saussure rejected the dominant organicist conception of language (1.1). For him, the primary subject matter of linguistics does not consist of linguistic forms developing in accordance with principles applying to forms of that type, like a species. It consists rather of signs which are radically arbitrary, so that their significance is determined only by the conventions of the historically constituted systems to which they belong. It follows, he thought, that the synchronic study of language is essentially one of social facts; that is, a study of the linguistic conventions and relations operative at a given time in virtue of which the signs of the system have the values that they do. But since he was concerned that the fundamental units should be concrete ones, he also thought that those conventions and relations ought to be psychologically real. So if language is a study of social facts, they are facts of social psychology, not ones which exclude psychology from the study of language. Where nineteenth-century linguistics had 'divorced the study of language from the study of mind' (Aarsleff 1967, 127), Saussure reintegrated the two.

As well as insisting that systems of signs form the primary subject matter of linguistics, he also tried to develop a novel way of studying them. This involved an appeal to a discipline which did not exist when he wrote, but which had 'a right to existence, a place staked out in advance' (*CLG*, 33, 16). That discipline is, of course, semiology; and one of the most difficult parts of his argument to evaluate is the attempt to derive fundamental distinctions and conclusions from the semiological principles proposed, beginning, of course, with the principle of the Arbitrariness of the Sign. But whatever the result of that evaluation, it is clear that Saussure's conception of semiology had a major impact on the development of structuralist thought in the human sciences in general. For, as Culler says,

> The importance of Saussure lies not simply in his contribution to linguistics *per se* but in the fact that he made what might otherwise have seemed a recondite and specialized discipline a major intellectual presence and model for other disciplines of the 'human sciences'. (1976, 53)

I shall have more to say about each of these themes in the remaining sections. But before embarking on detailed discussion it is worth speculating why Saussure did not think that his ideas on general linguistics were in a state fit for publication. Perhaps the main reason is that his arguments depended crucially on there being a determinate system to reconstruct. Yet not only does he not show how in detail to reconstruct such a system, but his theory as it stands leaves it very unclear indeed that it is even possible to do it in principle (7.2). Apart from his uncertainty about what to class as concrete and what as abstract (5.1) – the tensions in his system which lead him to treat sentences both as units of *parole* and as syntagms and hence as units of *langue* (5.3.2) – there is no reason to think that a determinate account of a sign's associative relations can be given. Indeed, as Ducrot has pointed out, there is every reason to think that it cannot:

> Each sign is [according to Saussure] therefore related to all those signs which delimit it, and which therefore constitute its paradigm. But Saussure was not able to extract a criterion of classification from his principle of negative limitation. The only phonic unities which interested him were in effect signifiers, that is unities which are already very complex, and which are as a result delimited by a very large number of neighboring signifiers. One must therefore accommodate within their paradign [= set of terms to which they are associatively related] a multitude of terms. . . . As a result, the ordering of terms within a paradigm becomes an impossible task, and furthermore it is not possible to classify them by relating them to each other. (1968, 74)

But without such an account it is impossible, on Saussure's theory, to determinately identify either the signs themselves or the system to which they belong. We can identify a sign only by identifying *all* its syntagmatic and associative relationships, and the system to which it belongs is simply the set of all such relationships among all its signs.

Another reason why Saussure might have been unhappy with his argument as it stood is that it leaves it unclear what the linguistics of *parole* could consist of. But unless *parole* can be systematically studied, then his theory leaves very little scope for historical linguistics. If the mechanisms of change always involve *parole*, then it is difficult to see what there is to say about them unless there is a linguistics of *parole*. As the text stands, the problem for someone who takes historical concerns seriously, as I believe Saussure did (1.1), is not that they have been relegated to a secondary position, but that it is quite unclear what a systematic study of them could be. The editors acknowledge that the absence of a linguistics of *parole* is regrettable, but go on to report: 'This study, which had been promised to the students of the third course, would undoubtedly have had a place of honor; why this promise could not be kept is too well known' (*CLG*, 10, xxxi). So here is a lacuna which Saussure intended to fill, and which urgently needs filling if a coherent methodology for diachronic linguistics is to be developed (7.1).

A third reason why Saussure might have felt his argument needed further development concerns its overall structure. If he indeed intended to base it on semiological principles, then surely a great deal more work needed to be done. For instance, as we saw, he claims that the whole mechanism of language depends on the principle of the Linearity of the Signifier, yet it is quite unclear how it does if it does (3.3). And there are many unresolved tensions implicit in the idea of a general science of signs (7.4).

7.1. The fundamental dichotomies

The crucial importance of the fundamental dichotomies is clear, for the distinction between *langue* and *parole*, on the one hand, and between synchronic and diachronic linguistics, on the other, is central to Saussure's claim that the primary object of study is a synchronic one of a system of signs. I have already described a number of unclarities in the way in which the first distinction is drawn (2.5), but how serious are these for Saussure's system as a whole?

7.1.1. Langue *and* parole

At least three unclarities have serious consequences. First, the issue raised by Culler over the conflicting conceptions of *langue* employed by Saussure brings into question his fundamental decision to ground his theory on the notion of a sign. We saw that the conflicting metaphors of *langue* as akin to Morse Code and to an orchestral score correspond roughly to Hjelmslev's distinction between schema and norm (2.4). But why does he have to choose between the former, more abstract, conception, and the latter, which includes the former? Part of the answer is that his theory of the sign as a double entity makes it very difficult to adopt the second conception. If one side of the double entity, the signified, is allocated to the representation of meaning, then the other can only represent the sign's 'vehicle' at one level of abstraction; and if there is only one level at which it can be represented, this has to be the most abstract. If he really wished to take norms into account and thus escape an excessively abstract conception of language, Saussure needed to cease to rest his theory on the conception of the sign as a double entity. Perhaps it does not follow strictly from the conception of the sign as a double entity that it cannot be represented on many more or less abstract levels. But there seems to be little doubt that he did not explore this possibility and, faithful to the conception of a sign as double entity, maintained that a *langue* is a system for correlating *two* distinct orders of differences, one phonic and one psychological (*CLG*, 166, 120).

Second, the way in which Saussure defines *parole* means, we saw, that it is at best an ill-defined rag-bag of what is left when *langue* is subtracted from *langage* and at worst not defined at all, since it is never clear precisely what does belong to *langage* (2.1.3). If taken seriously, the implication that because of its very heterogeneity *parole* provides no subject matter worthy of study leads to a very narrow conception of the scope of linguistics. Furthermore, as I said above, the failure to articulate an account of *parole* also puts a stop to the development of diachronic linguistics, since the mechanisms of change always involve *parole*.

Third, the failure to show that *langue* is passive, in the sense that the individual who acquires it by participating in communicative interchanges plays no part in its acquisition, threatens to undermine Saussure's principle of radical arbitrariness (2.1.2). If individuals are not wholly passive, then the possibility that their language faculty plays some role in the process cannot be ruled out. Just how active that role might be is no doubt a matter for argument, but the failure to exclude it threatens to wreck the exclusively semiological approach. As things stand, Saussure has to concede the existence of at least one linguistic universal, the fact that all languages consist of systems of signs formally constituted by their syntagmatic and associative relations. Unless this can be shown to follow from fundamental semiological principles, which I have argued it cannot, then Saussure has, on his own account, to concede *some* contribution by the language faculty

(3.3, 7.4). Moreover, given the failure of his argument about passivity, that contribution could be very great indeed, as Chomsky has argued it in fact is (1965; 1966; 1969).

7.1.2. Diachronic and synchronic

The implications of the unclarities in the way in which the distinction between synchronic and diachronic linguistics is drawn for Saussure's system as a whole might seem less serious than those we have been looking at. His arguments that the primary linguistic study is a synchronic study of *langue* have come to be so widely accepted that it is genuinely difficult to imagine how anyone could have supposed anything else to be the case. Yet this extraordinary achievement cannot obscure the fact that Saussure did not succeed in delineating the subject matter of diachronic linguistics; and, of course, if its subject matter is not well defined, then, to the degree that it is not, so must the subject matter of synchronic linguistics be ill defined also.

We saw that the first model of diachronic linguistics, that of two intersecting temporal axes, which implies that we are dealing with one and the same thing studied from different points of view, is clearly unsatisfactory. For synchronic linguistics is actually idiosynchronic, whilst items existing at the same time may be studied diachronically (4.5). This strongly suggests that the preferred analogy is with chess. But this analogy too, we saw, seems to have serious drawbacks from Saussure's point of view. In chess the time taken to effect transitions from one state to another has no significance, so that the history of the game can be represented as a series of non-overlapping states with no intervals between them. But Saussure thinks that changes in languages are not like that, since there may be periods of time in which there is no stable state. In such a case, Saussure would argue, the only possible study is a diachronic one. But apart from the fact that it is difficult to see what this could be, given his account of *parole* as it stands, the claim that no synchronic description is possible in such cases entails that one cannot describe the *langue* internalised by the speakers of the language, in spite of the fact that it is a fundamental principle of his theory that there must be one. In short, at this point there is a totally unresolved hiatus.

7.2. Language and determinacy

It is, of course, a fundamental principle of Saussure's system that there is no *parole* without a corresponding *langue*, because signs are constituted by their position in the latter. But is there a determinate way of identifying the underlying system and of relating a given sign to it? Ducrot, as we saw, argued that there is not. The number of signs with which a given sign can be related associatively and syntagmatically is indefinitely large, so that it is not in principle possible to describe them all. But even if it were, it is not clear that the resulting system would be determinate, for reasons given by Quine.[1]

According to Quine's indeterminacy thesis,[2] 'manuals for translating one language into another can be set up in divergent ways, all compatible with the totality of speech dispositions, yet incompatible with one another' (1960, 27). Indeterminacy arises because there is no sense in which one manual can be said to be right and the other wrong in the areas in which they diverge. Moreover, the indeterminacy is not simply a matter of underdetermination,[3] for though the competing translation manuals are indeed underdetermined by the data, the distinctions they make are purely products of the respective theories, and so in neither case reflect antecedent distinctions:

> ...two translators might develop independent manuals of translation, both of them compatible with all dispositions to speech behavior, and yet one translator would offer translations that the other would reject. My position was that either manual could be useful, but as to which was right and which wrong there was no fact of the matter. (Quine 1977, 167)

Quine's thesis is vividly illustrated by considering the problems of a linguist involved in radical translation, i.e., translation of a language which has not been translated before. The point of concentrating on this case is that it is one in which the linguist has to adopt a naturalistic and behaviouristic account of meaning, since there is no alternative.

In such a situation the linguist would, Quine argues, be able to translate native observation sentences,[4] such as 'Gagavi' standardly uttered when rabbits are present but not when other animals are. He is able to translate this sentence because he is able to observe the kinds of conditions in which native speakers assent to/dissent from it, and can hence, subject to inductive uncertainty, infer what their dispositions to assent to/dissent from 'Gagavi' are.

Translation of this sort, Quine argues, 'can be objective.... But the linguist's bold further step, in which he imposes his own object-positing pattern without special warrant, is taken when he equates the native expression or any part of it with the *term* "rabbit" ' (1969, 2). This is a bold step indeed, because

> given that a native sentence says that a so-and-so is present, and given that the sentence is true when and only when a rabbit is present, it by no means follows that the so-and-so are rabbits. They might be all the various temporal segments of rabbits. They might be all the integral or undetached parts of rabbits. (Ibid.)

It might seem that we could easily decide between these alternatives by identifying the native's sign for identity. But that, Quine argues, is an illusion:

> For if one workable overall system of [analytical] hypotheses provides for translating a given native expression into 'is the same as', perhaps another equally workable but systematically different system would translate that native expression rather into something like 'belongs with'. Then when in the native language we try to ask 'Is this *gagavi* the same as that?' we could well be asking 'Does this *gagavi* belong with that?' (Ibid., 33)

Quine's own comment on this example is instructive. The argument depends on the fact that differing translations of a given term can be compensated for by adjustments elsewhere in the system. We could put the same point in Saussurean terms as follows: Differing analyses of, or ways of segmenting, a complex term are possible provided that (i) the differences between the two analyses are compensated for elsewhere; and (ii) differing sets of associative and syntagmatic relations are proposed in the two cases. This is a conclusion which Saussure would not welcome, since it totally undermines the assumption that there is a determinate system. Yet it is far from clear that he can escape it, for, behaviourism apart, there are a number of striking similarities between Quine's approach to the study of language and Saussure's.

First, Quine writes: 'With Dewey I hold that knowledge, mind, and meaning are part of the same world that they have to do with, and that they are to be studied in the same empirical spirit that animates natural science. There is no place for prior philosophy' (ibid., 26). Whilst Saussure cannot be unreservedly associated with this naturalistic approach if it is held to encompass behaviourism, there is no doubt that he would have embraced many aspects of it. For example, he criticised the *Port Royal Grammar* for its *a priori* approach; poured scorn on the approach of Schleicher which 'led to methods of reasoning which would have caused astonishment in other sciences' (*CLG*, 17, 4); and insisted that linguistics is concerned with concrete rather than abstract entities (5.1). In other words, for him linguistics is a science with its own subject matter.

Second, Quine's objections to what he calls 'uncritical semantics' bear a striking resemblance to Saussure's objections to the idea that language is a nomenclature (3.1). For Quine, uncritical semantics is 'the myth of a museum in which the exhibits are meanings and the words are labels' (1969, 27). So, like Saussure, Quine objects to the idea that words stand for predetermined ideas. Indeed, in objecting to the myth of a museum Quine is objecting not only to mentalism, but also to the identification of meanings with objects of any kind 'whether one assumes that object to be an idea, a proposition, a physical body, or a Platonic form' (Gibson 1982, 32).

Third, not only does Quine reject nomenclaturism but, again like Saussure, insists that meanings are language-dependent: 'Meanings are, first and foremost, meanings of language. Language is a social art which we all acquire on the evidence solely of other people's overt behavior under publicly recognizable circumstances' (1969, 26). Not surprisingly in view of this, Quine, as well as Saussure, subscribes to a version of semantic holism according to which the unit of meaning is not a sentence but a language.

Thus it seems that the key steps on which Quine's conclusion depends are ones that Saussure would accept. In particular:

(i) Complex terms need to be segmented if we are to analyse a language

(ii) There is nothing extralinguistic which determines which of the many possible ways of doing this is correct

(iii) Any analysis/segmentation uncovers a system

It is tempting to argue against the indeterminacy thesis that any analysis has to reconstruct the phonology, morphology, syntax, and semantics of a language as well as yield interpretations for sentences in context that are pragmatically acceptable, and that it is simply inconceivable that there should be radically different ways of doing this. But whether or not such an argument is plausible, it is not available to Saussure. What plausibility the argument has depends on its being true that the various subsystems of a language are subject to strong formal constraints. But according to Saussure's theory the only formal constraint is the weak one that the elements being analysed be related to each other both associatively and syntagmatically. The strong version of the principle of the Arbitrariness of the Sign to which Saussure subscribes rules out the existence of any other constraints, formal or otherwise. Indeed, it seems that in Saussure's case analyses are even less constrained than in Quine's. For the latter, we at least reach bedrock with the dispositions to assent/dissent of the native speakers, whereas for Saussure there is no corresponding constraint.

But if, given his overall assumptions, Saussure's method cannot in principle yield a determinate description of the underlying system, then he has clearly failed to achieve his fundamental aim of identifying the object of linguistics. And, as Ducrot points out, if the underlying system cannot be identified, then neither can its components, given that they have to be defined relationally.

7.3. Language as social fact

As we shall see, the question of Saussure's commitment to the kind of social realism espoused by Durkheim does not admit of a simple answer, since there are important individualistic strands in Saussure's thought. But before tackling this question, we had better ask first just what was Saussure's relation to Durkheim. Some have argued that it is not clear that there was one.

7.3.1. Saussure and Durkheim

We saw earlier that Mounin claims that the important sociological dimension in Saussure's thought is one which has to be defined in relation to Durkheim (1.1). However, Mounin argues, this is not a straightforward matter; though they were more or less exact contemporaries, they did not meet. The discussion of social facts in Durkheim's *Rules of Sociological Method* makes only a passing reference to language, and though in his article on sociology and the social sciences in the *Revue Philosophique* in 1903 Durkheim proposed that language should be studied sociologically as a social institution, this hardly shows, Mounin concedes, that Durkheim directly influenced Saussure. For though the latter also invokes the metaphor of language as a social institution, so too had Whitney, and Saussure had certainly read him.

In fact two questions need to be asked which are never very clearly distinguished in Mounin's discussion: Did Saussure know of Durkheim's ideas? Did those ideas positively shape his thought?

Though Durkheim is never mentioned in *CLG*, there is ample evidence that Saussure knew of Durkheim's work. He corresponded regularly with Meillet, a former pupil of his who became a professor at the Collège de France in 1906 and who had argued that language fits Durkheim's definition, since it is independent of particular users, but affects them causally. There is also the evidence of Doroszewski, who wrote that he knew 'from a reliable source that Saussure followed with deep interest the philosophical debate between Durkheim and Tarde' (1933, 90). And in 1957 he revealed his source: Louis Caille, one of Saussure's pupils whose notes formed the basis for *CLG*.

Even without this evidence, it would be difficult to believe that Saussure was not aware of Durkheim's ideas. The dispute between him and Tarde referred to above was carried on in journals for nearly a decade, culminating in a famous public debate in 1903. It would be extraordinary if an original thinker in search of analogies on which to base his account of language had overlooked such a debate or was not aware of the Durkheimian concept of a social fact (Sampson 1980, 48).

But if the answer to the question whether Saussure knew about Durkheim's views is clear, the question of the latter's influence is much more complex. In this connection the debate between Durkheim and Tarde is instructive.

Durkheim was a social realist;[5] that is, he believed that there are social facts and that, moreover, explanations of them are not generally reducible without remainder to facts about human individuals. Such facts constitute the subject matter of sociology, which is distinct from psychology precisely because it has its own subject matter:

> ...one is forced to admit that these specific facts reside in the society itself that produces them and not in its parts – namely its members. In this sense therefore they lie outside the consciousness of individuals as such, in the same way as the distinctive features of life lie outside the chemical substances that make up a living organism. (Durkheim 1982, 39)

Thus for him to treat suicide as a social fact is

> to consider [it], not as an aggregate of individual acts, but as a patterned phenomenon. If '...the suicides committed in a given society during a given period of time are taken as a whole', we find that 'this total is not simply a sum of independent units, a collective total, but is itself a new fact *sui generis*, with its own unity, individuality, and consequently its own nature'. The suicide rate remains fairly stable in any given society from year to year.... This stability affirms, according to Durkheim, that we are in the presence of a social fact. For we can be certain that the individuals who figure in the suicide rate in one year are not the same as those who compose it in the next. There must be certain social influences acting upon all these individuals. (Giddens 1978, 43; the quotation is from Durkheim 1952, 46)

But even if it is true that the explanation of social facts cannot be reduced to psychological facts, a positive characterisation of them is clearly needed.

The first chapter of Durkheim's methodological treatise, *The Rules of Sociological Method*, is devoted to a discussion of this question: It concludes with the following account:

> A social fact is any way of acting, whether fixed or not, capable of exercising over the individual an external constraint; or: which is general over the

whole of a given society whilst having an existence of its own, independent of its individual manifestations. (1982, 59)

This seems to propose two characterisations of a social fact, one in terms of the notions of externality and constraint, and one in terms of generality with independence from any individual instantiation.

By 'externality' Durkheim seems to have meant independence from any particular individual's will. Many norms or conventions are, he argues, external in this sense. For though I may have internalised them, 'it is not I who have prescribed these duties; I have received them through education' (ibid., 50). Unlike habits, which rule us from within, 'social beliefs and practices act on us from the outside' (p. 44). Thus church members find their beliefs and practices ready-made. As well as being external, a social fact constrains individuals in the sense that it imposes itself on them independently of their will. It is true that in consenting to it they may not feel any sense of constraint, but its existence manifests itself as soon as they try to resist. So, according to the first of the two characterisations of a social fact, it exists independently of the will of any of the individuals it constrains.

The second characterisation of a social fact retains the idea of externality, now defined as 'independence from individual manifestations'. By 'generality' Durkheim simply refers to diffusion of the social fact within a group, so that it has a wider extension than facts of individual psychology, but a narrower one than facts of biology. Clearly, this characterisation is not equivalent to the first, since it omits reference to the notion of constraint. One reason that Durkheim gives for adopting it rather than the first is methodological; constraint can be hard to identify (Durkheim 1982, 57). Another is, Lukes argues, that Durkheim wanted to count far too many different things as instances of constraint for the concept to be useful from his point of view (1973, 14). But though this is a plausible criticism of Durkheim's use of the term, it is not for that reason that he proposed the second characterisation. On the contrary, the two characterisations are, according to him, linked by the fact that 'if a mode of behavior existing outside the consciousness of individuals becomes general, it can only do so by bringing pressure on them' (1982, 57). In other words, the second characterisation is *de facto* equivalent to the first, because the requisite kind of generality with independence will obtain only when there is constraint, whether or not we can identify the precise form the constraint takes. There is, therefore, no need to mention constraint; when the conditions mentioned in the second characterisation obtain, it will be present. So, though not mentioned, it is important; and when Durkheim wrote the preface to the second edition of the *Rules* in 1901 he continued to emphasise the importance of it: '...this is what is most essential in the idea of social constraint. For all that it implies is that collective ways of acting and thinking possess a reality existing outside individuals who, at every moment, conform to them' (1982, 44). Though there undoubtedly are problems with Durkheim's employment of the notion of constraint, it can hardly be omitted altogether from his account of social facts.

Not surprisingly, publication of the *Rules* provoked a controversy about the nature and existence of social facts, which was pursued at times with great acrimony. One of Durkheim's leading critics, Tarde, was a methodological individualist and hence believed that social facts have to be explained ultimately in terms of facts about individuals. As Mill put it, 'Human beings in society have no properties but those which are derived from, and may be resolved into the laws of individual man' (1875, 469). Tarde argued that imitation plays a major role in accounting for the uniformity of social behavior, and so proposed a distinctively individualistic account of social facts. But where does Saussure stand in all of this? Is he a social realist or a methodological individualist?[6]

7.3.2. The issue

To begin with, an important point is that methodological individualism is, as its name suggests, a methodological and not an ontological thesis, so that a proponent of it could perfectly well allow that statements about social individuals are not logically reducible to ones about human individuals (Danto 1973, 321; MacDonald & Pettit 1981, 106ff). What the methodological individualist is committed to maintaining is rather:

(i) Social facts have to be explained causally in terms of facts
     about individuals, and not vice versa
(ii) Though there may be explanations of social facts in terms
     of other social facts, these are not ultimate (Danto 1973, 322)

So, if H is a predicate of human individuals and C one of social
individuals, then according to the methodological individualist
an ultimate explanation will contain laws of the form (1a) but
no laws of the form (1b):

(1a) $Vx\, Vy\, (Hx \rightarrow Cy)$
(1b) $Vx\, Vy\, (Cy \rightarrow Hx)$

In other words, the explanation will contain laws which account
for the properties of social individuals in terms of those of human individuals, but will not contain laws which account for the
properties of human individuals in terms of those of social individuals. By contrast, social realists will maintain that *sometimes*
ultimate explanations will contain laws of the form (1b) – though
they can of course concede that often ultimate explanations contain only laws of the form (1a) – and so give themselves less to
prove than methodological individualists (D'Agostino 1986, 15).
    It is not thus far clear what counts as a predicate of an indi-
vidual. However, it is clear both that this is a crucial issue and
that if a relatively relaxed view is taken of what counts, the victory
of methodological individualists is going to be too easy to make
their thesis interesting. They might, for instance, claim that an
explanation of the success of a certain party in an election in
terms of the high turnout of its members is an individualist one,
even though the predicate 'is a member of party x' used in that
explanation remains unreduced. So it is necessary to place some
restriction on H; for instance, that it is a predicate which involves
no essential reference to a social individual or event and does
not ascribe to its bearer an irreducibly social attitude. Whether
this suggestion is the right way of making the restriction is a
moot point, but it is clear that what the restriction has to do is
to ensure that in ultimate explanations the only laws involved
are ones which, in Mill's phrase, are 'resolved into the laws of
individual man' (7.3.1). A restriction of this sort would seem to
be acceptable to methodological individualists. Watkins, for instance, writes:

> Society is a system of unobservable relationships between individuals whose interaction produces certain measurable sociological phenomena. We can apprehend an unobservable social system by reconstructing it theoretically from what is known of individual dispositions, beliefs and relationships. (1973, 165)

Presumably the dispositions in question, whether ones possessed by everyone, e.g., acquisitiveness, or ones possessed by only some of us, e.g., bravery, are the subject matter of individual rather than social psychology. Otherwise it is hard to see what force there could be to the claim that something unobservable had been reconstructed from something observable.

7.3.3. Saussure's individualism

Recalling that for Durkheim the characteristics of a social fact are generality (but not universality) and external constraint, meaning by the latter 'independence of any particular individual's will', then Saussure's characterisation of facts about *langue* is strikingly reminiscent of Durkheim. Such facts are general in the relevant sense and involve constraint, since according to Saussure 'the individual does not have the power to change a sign in any way once it has become established in the linguistic community' (*CLG*, 101, 69). Indeed, we saw that in the course of trying to explain why languages are so stable he goes even further, claiming: 'No individual, even if he willed it, could modify in any way at all the choice that has been made; and what is more, the community itself cannot control so much as a single word; it is bound to the existing language' (*CLG*, 104, 71).

The reasons why this is so are, Saussure argues, connected with the fact that language is a heritage from preceding generations (3.4). Language is checked by the weight of the collectivity, since 'it blends with the life of society'; but it is checked also by time: 'These two are inseparable. At every moment solidarity with the past checks freedom of choice. We say *man* and *dog* because our predecessors said *man* and *dog*' (*CLG*, 108, 74). But if no one invents his or her language, and indeed passively assimilates it, then it would seem to follow that there cannot be an individualistic explanation of why, for instance, the plural of 'goose' in modern English is 'geese'. For facts about the language I speak cannot be explained in terms of anything I have done,

since I am powerless to change the language I speak. It is something I did not invent but acquired passively by participating in
exchanges. But the same is true of my ancestors, and of their
ancestors, and so on. So it would seem that Saussure is committed
to claiming that

(1) No individualistic explanation of why 'geese' is the plural of
     'goose' in modern English can be given

But what then are we to make of the actual explanation he
gives of the way in which this in fact came about? I described
this in detail earlier (4.2); the essential points are these. In modern English 'goose' is one of a number of nouns with plurals
marked by a specific vowel change. How these nouns came to
be this way involves three previous stages, the transitions between
which were brought about by phonetic changes that had nothing
to do with the plural *per se*. At the first stage the plural was
marked by the addition of a final *i* to the singular form, so that
the language contained the pair *gōs:gōsi*. Then, as a result of a
phonetic change which occurred whenever *i* followed a stressed
syllable, the contrasting pair became *gōs:gēsi*. The language now
made available in this sort of case, two ways of marking the
plural: the addition of a final *i* and the contrast between *o* and
e. Finally, at the third stage, as a result of the fall of the final *i*,
the language contained the pair *gōs:gēs*.

Now, if all the transitions involved were of this kind, then it
would be hard to resist Saussure's conclusion that the diachronic
facts responsible for changes in the way the plural is marked
were in no way *directed* at bringing them about; they were simply
the unintentional by-product of changes in the phonetic system.
Indeed, as we saw (4.2), one of the points that Saussure wished
to underline was that since the phonetic changes responsible for
the evolution of the various ways of marking the plural were not
designed to bring them about, an account of that evolution cannot be teleological: 'Speakers did not wish to pass from one
system of relations to another' (*CLG*, 121, 84). But, of course,
the fact that the explanation is not teleological does not mean
that it cannot be individualistic; one has only to think of the
Darwinian theory of evolution, with which Saussure's account
shares some similarities, to see that. Perhaps, for instance, the
transition from Stage 2 to Stage 3 (i.e., from *gōs:gēsi* to *gōs:gēs*)
came about because some speakers omitted to pronounce the

final *i* and others followed suit; since there was no loss in the expressive power of the language involved, there was no reason why the variation should not become entrenched.

This is of course speculative. But it is consistent with Saussure's claim that it is 'in speaking (*parole*) that the germ of all change is to be found' (*CLG*, 138, 98). Moreover, it does draw attention to the fact that an individualistic explanation need not be teleological; things might have changed as a result of things speakers did, even though what they did was not designed to bring the changes about. As Popper has pointed out, the route taken by a path can be the result of innumerable individual acts, none of which was done with the intention that the path should follow the route it does.

Indeed, though it is speculative, the explanation is no worse than one Saussure himself gives. This concerns the change in the conjugation of the German copula in the sixteenth century, which involved the replacement of *was* by *war*, so that the conjugation *ich was*, *wir waren* became *ich war*, *wir waren* ('I was', 'We were'):

> Some speakers, influenced by *waren*, created *war* through analogy; this was a fact of speaking; the new form, repeated many times and accepted by the community, became a fact of language. But not all innovations of speaking (*parole*) have the same success, and so long as they remain individual they may be ignored. (*CLG*, 138, 98)

So it would seem that, after all, Saussure ought to be willing to concede that

(ii) An individualistic explanation why 'geese' is the plural of 'goose' can be given, though it is not, of course, teleological

This conclusion, on reflection, might not seem all that surprising. It is certainly not self-evident that the characteristics of social facts, generality and constraint, cannot be explained individualistically.[7] Consider Saussure's own question, raised when he introduces the distinction between *langue* and *parole*, 'How does the social crystallization of language come about?' (*CLG*, 29, 13) – that is, how does it come to be the case that members of the same linguistic community have broadly similar representations of their *langue*? His own answer seems to be individualistic

(2.1.2). A group of people came to have similar representations because they talk to each other, and as a result of their efforts to interpret each other, 'impressions that are perceptibly the same for all are made on the minds of speakers' (*CLG*, 29, 13). Though short on detail, this account is individualistic. For Saussure, *langue* is the product of face-to-face communicative interchanges between individuals, each of whom, as a result of these interchanges, ends up with a similar representation of it. The collective existence of these representations is then a social fact because of the explanation of how they are acquired and the role they play in further exchanges. For since this explanation requires two or more individuals, it presupposes generality, one of the characteristics of social facts mentioned by Durkheim. Moreover, it guarantees externality, i.e., independence of any particular individual's will, another of the characteristics he mentions. As for constraint, this arises for Saussure, as we saw, because of the way in which language is acquired, its widespread diffusion, the effect of transmission over time, etc. (3.4.1). The collective force of all these factors makes it very difficult for the individual not to conform to the linguistic practices of other members of the community.

7.3.4. Saussure as social theorist

The account above is an individualistic one. There was no point at which it seemed to be necessary to invoke the idea of a collective mind and its representations, unless indeed that is simply a shorthand way of talking about representations in the minds of individuals within the community, in explaining how the social crystallisation of language came about. Nevertheless, it is not clear that Saussure could accept that a thoroughgoing individualistic explanation of all aspects of language change and language acquisition is possible. There are two reasons why this is so.

First, consider the explanation Saussure gives of the change of conjugation of the German copula in the sixteenth century, in which *ich was, wir waren* became *ich war, wir waren*. As we saw, Saussure's explanation is that some speakers created *war* by analogy with *waren*, and others followed suit, so that eventually the new form displaced the old one. Now, for this to happen speakers must have had beliefs about the form of the first person plural in order to use it as a model for the first person singular. However, it is difficult to see how such beliefs could be ascribed to them without using predicates which refer to the German language as it was then constituted. But since it is far from clear that these predicates are in the relevant sense individualistic, i.e., ones which do not make an essential reference to a social individual or ascribe to its bearer an irreducibly social attitude, it is far from clear that this is an individualistic explanation. To be sure, the only agents involved are human individuals; there is no suggestion that social individuals or facts are themselves *agents*. However, the human individuals would not have acted as they did had they not had beliefs about social entities. So what we have is not a thoroughgoing individualistic explanation.

It might, however, be objected that this is not an ultimate explanation, and that reference to social entities would be eliminated in such an explanation. But on what grounds can it be said not to be ultimate? It surely cannot be because it is incomplete in the sense that it does not explain how the German language came to be in that state at that time. It is hard to see how any explanation could be anything other than incomplete in this sense. Presumably the point is that the very existence of any laws, rules, or conventions invoked can be explained individualistically, so that they are only intermediate generalisations. For instance, it might be argued that it was only a convention that the first person plural of the German copula was *wir waren* and that the notion of a convention can be analysed individualistically, thanks to an analysis proposed by Lewis.

According to Lewis,

> Conventions are regularities in action, or in action and belief, which are arbitrary but perpetuate themselves because they serve some sort of common interest. Past conformity breeds future conformity because it gives one a reason to go on conforming; but there is some alternative regularity which could have served instead. (1975, 4)[8]

In other words, a convention is an arbitrary beneficial regularity. For instance, driving on the left in England is a convention because though the regularity is arbitrary – we could have driven on the right – it is beneficial, since it is in everyone's interest to drive on the same side of the road. And it does seem true that past conformity provides a reason for future conformity. But precisely how does it do so?

A key part of Lewis's answer to this question involves the notion of mutual knowledge. There is mutual knowledge that q when everyone knows that q, everyone knows that everyone knows that q, and so on. Now, according to Lewis not only does everyone drive on the left, but it is mutually known that this is so; moreover, it is mutually known both that the belief that everyone else does it gives each individual a reason also to do it, and that there is an alternative beneficial regularity. Thus, because of mutual knowledge everyone can replicate everyone else's reasoning, and so everyone can see that everyone else has a reason to conform. So the mutual-knowledge 'condition ensures stability. If anyone tries to replicate another's reasoning, perhaps including the replication of his own reasoning, . . . the result will reinforce rather than subvert his expectation of conformity to R' (Lewis 1975, 6). In other words, every member of P's beliefs about what everyone else in P is going to do reinforces what would otherwise be a weak reason for personally conforming to a regularity R.[9]

However, the appeal to mutual knowledge to explain the perpetuation of the regularity makes it questionable whether this is a genuinely individualistic explanation. For in the explanation of how an individual coordinates his or her actions with those of everyone else, it is necessary to attribute to everyone both a belief about what everyone else believes and a belief about a general preference for general conformity. In each case, predicates involving an ineliminable reference to other members of a group are involved.

The second reason for doubting whether Saussure would accept that a thoroughgoing individualist explanation of language change can be given is that for him it is axiomatic that there is no *parole* without *langue*. Hence any explanatory theory of *parole* will presuppose, or draw on, a theory of *langue*; this is the whole point of the metaphor of the platform on which the theoretical study of language stands (2.1.3). Note that Saussure's account does not attribute agency to *langue* – the only agents of language change, according to him, are human individuals. His point is that one cannot explain why individuals speak as they do without ascribing to them beliefs about a *langue*.

In conclusion, three points. If the methodological individualists' main point is that human individuals are agents but social individuals are not, then Saussure has no quarrel with them as far as I can see. However, if the methodological individualists want also to insist that social facts can be explained without attributing to human individuals attitudes towards social individuals, then Saussure cannot agree with them. But even if Saussure is not a methodological individualist for this reason, that does not mean that he is committed to denying that individualistic explanations are ever appropriate in linguistics. As we saw, a denial of methodological individualism commits one only to the claim that sometimes individualistic explanations are inadequate.

7.4. Language, science, and signs

Saussure's conception of semiology raises two main questions. First, to what extent was his own approach to linguistics semiological, and how successful was it? Second, what impact did his conception of semiology have on the development of both semiology itself and other disciplines? Clearly, the second of these questions is a topic for a book in its own right; we shall here concentrate on the first.[10]

There is no doubt that Saussure attached great importance to a semiological approach to linguistics. Shortly after introducing his conception of semiology as '*a science that studies the life of signs within society*' (*CLG*, 33, 16) he writes, 'I wish merely to call attention to one thing: if I have succeeded in assigning linguistics a place among the sciences, it is because I have related it to semiology' (ibid.). One reason why he insisted on this relation was no doubt to distance himself from the organicist conceptions of the comparativists, which he rejected totally (1.1). Another was that doing this underlined his social conception of language by making it the subject matter of social psychology. But perhaps the most important reason was that by comparing a language with other semiological systems it would be possible to see what were its essential and its non-essential features most clearly:

> ...to me the language problem is mainly semiological, and all developments derive their significance from that important fact. If we are to discover the true nature of language we must learn what it has in common with all other semiological systems; lin-

guistic forces that seem very important at first glance (e.g., the role of the vocal apparatus) will receive only secondary consideration if they serve only to set language apart from the other systems. (*CLG*, 34, 17)

If we study a language from the point of view of individual psychology, or indeed of sociology, we are likely, Saussure thought, to concentrate on more or less contingent features and overlook the fact that it is a system of signs – its most important characteristic. Only adoption of the semiological perspective will enable us to see this clearly and to concentrate on the key question. What are the essential features of such systems?

From this point of view, the way to begin the study of language is to develop the theory of signs, to describe the principles that hold for all signs and sign systems, and then to derive a description of linguistic sign systems from the theory and the principles. It might be argued that the text of *CLG* should not have been organised so that it began with the distinction between *langue* and *parole* as though that were something ultimate. The text should rather have begun with the theory and principles of semiology, from which the distinction between *langue* and *parole* should have been derived.[11]

However, if this was Saussure's strategy, it is surely a questionable one. To begin with, it takes it for granted that different sign systems have something interesting in common, in spite of the fact that the examples given are very diverse, viz. 'a system of writing, the alphabet of deaf-mutes, symbolic rites, polite formulas, military signals, etc.' (*CLG*, 33, 16). In fact, the first of these is, according to Saussure, a secondary and parasitic system, whilst the second, since it is alphabetic, has no morphology or syntax of its own. Semaphore, one type of military signal, is like the deaf alphabet in this respect, whilst naval signals using flags, another type of military signal, are, according to Saussure's own principles, unlike linguistic signifiers in that they are not constrained by the principle of linearity (3.3). Symbolic rites and polite formulas, unlike words, do not enter into many interesting syntagmatic relationships, so that they are not obviously part of productive systems, i.e., ones with indefinitely many 'utterances'. This may be so because they themselves are often more like utterances than like words – e.g., greetings, farewells, congratulations, etc.[12]

Clearly, the question of the ways in which linguistic signs are special is of crucial importance for Saussure's argument, yet it surfaces only once in *CLG*, when the question of the extent to which other signs are arbitrary is raised. No doubt Saussure is right to insist that though polite formulas may be based on natural expressions they are nevertheless fixed by rule, for it is often specified who ought to use them in whose presence and when. However, the crucial comparison is not with rules of this sort but with the rules that define the *content* of the formulas: Do the formulas form systems within which they are related by analogues of associative and syntagmatic relations? *Prima facie*, many non-verbal signs do not form systems, but consist rather of exaggerated ways of doing what one might be doing anyway. Take what Goffman calls body gloss.

> In our own middle-class society, for example, there is a standardized little Scarsdale smile, held over-long, . . . 'transfixed' so that throughout the whole period of an offender's behaviour he will be accorded a sign that no offence is being taken, that no contest is involved, and that sympathy is present for whatever alignment to the situation he chooses to take. (1972, 156)

In these sorts of cases conventionalisation seems to consist of nothing more than a stylised and somewhat exaggerated way of doing what one might be doing naturally. It is difficult to see what the system is or could be.

Anyway, if Saussure's aim was to discover what is essential to language by eliminating anything which is not common to all sign systems, then he was clearly in very great danger of having only a few very abstract characteristics left with which to characterise it or, at worst, nothing at all. Moreover, such a strategy is not obviously consistent with the idea that a language is an autonomous social institution of a quite special kind, so it is not surprising that there is a certain tension in Saussure's account leading him to vacillate between two quite different positions. According to the first, which I have been discussing, the strategy is to begin with the laws of semiology and to derive the characteristics of *langue* from them. But according to the second, the way to proceed is to study *langue* as a semiological institution and then to take stock and see what light this study throws on semiology in general.

The attraction of the second position for Saussure is clear from his insistence that language is the most important of the semiological systems, and that 'to determine the exact place of semiology is the task of the psychologist. The task of the linguist is to find out what makes language a special system within the mass of semiological data' (*CLG*, 33, 16). Moreover, 'Linguists have been going around in circles: language, better than anything else, offers a basis for understanding the semiological problem; but language must, to put it correctly, be studied in itself' (*CLG*, 34, 16). Indeed, much of the time it would seem to be this second modest strategy that is in fact followed. Saussure's analysis of the sign, for instance, questionable though it may be as a study of linguistic signs, would be even more so if it was meant as one of signs in general: The conception of the signifier as an acoustic image seems quite inappropriate for mathematics, the deaf alphabet, semaphore, etc. So what his account of synchronic linguistics starts with is, in effect, not an analysis of signs, but one of linguistic signs.

I suggested earlier that, whatever his intentions, much of Saussure's argument does not depend on his commitment to the first of the two strategies distinguished above, which bases the argument on the theory of signs in general, but at most on the more modest one, which is semiological to the extent that it studies languages as a species of sign system but makes little or no appeal to the theory of signs in general (1.1). This, of course, does not rule out the possibility of using the results of that study as a model for the study of other sign systems, which incidentally would seem to be all that is necessary for the kind of application to social anthropology of the work of structural linguistics envisaged by Lévi-Strauss (1977, 31).

Certainly it would have to be conceded that if the first strategy was Saussure's, its theoretical base was very restricted indeed. Apart from the scepticism I expressed about whether all sign systems have anything in common at all, and apart from the fact that it is hardly plausible to take his analysis of the sign as one of signs in general, his argument rests on just two primordial principles. But of these the second, the Linear Nature of the Signifier, on which the whole mechanism of language is said to depend, is evidently not a general semiological principle applicable to sign systems of every kind. For that matter, the first principle, the Arbitrariness of the Sign, is not obviously so, either, if the qualification 'radically' is taken seriously. However, it might seem attractive at this point to make a definitional move and restrict semiology to the study of sign systems whose signs are arbitrary. And though Saussure does not in fact do this, he comes quite close to doing so by arguing that semiology's 'main concern will still be the whole group of systems grounded on the arbitrariness of the sign' (CLG, 100, 68). Even so, there are, he acknowledges, degrees of arbitrariness; for instance, gestures and symbols, such as the scales of justice, are not wholly arbitrary. But presumably then the strong version of the principle needed for language will not be appropriate in these cases (according to the strong principle, linguistic signs are wholly, i.e., radically, arbitrary). So even if the scope of semiology is restricted to systems which are to some degree arbitrary, it is not clear that there is just one precisely specified principle of arbitrariness which applies to them all.

And Barthes's claim that other semiological systems are, as it were, parasitic on language has to be answered; this is a point that he makes very forcibly:

> It is true that objects, images and patterns of behaviour can signify, and do so on a large scale, but never autonomously; every semiological system has its linguistic admixture. Where there is a visual substance, for example, the meaning is confirmed by being duplicated in a linguistic message ... so that at least a part of the iconic message is, in terms of structural relationship, either redundant or taken up by the linguistic system. (Barthes 1967, 10)

Of course if this is so, then, as Barthes points out, other semiological systems cannot be independent of language. But if they are not, there is no generalised semiology which could provide the theoretical starting point for a study of language.

Moreover, not only does the first strategy have a thin theoretical base, but its implementation leaves a lot to be desired. As we saw, Saussure never establishes that signs are radically arbitrary in the sense of being totally unmotivated; indeed, many possible forms of motivation are simply not discussed (3.2). Connected, the failure to show that language acquisition is wholly passive opens up the possibility that the language faculty itself plays a substantial role in language learning (7.1). Third, the attempt to derive from the principle of Linearity a theoretical justification for the claim that the only linguistically relevant relations are associative and syntagmatic ones not only fails, but leaves one wondering how it ever could have been expected to account for associative relations, which are *non*-linear by definition. Fourth, system, a key idea for the development of Saussure's argument, is treated as a species of arbitrariness – relative arbitrariness – whereas it is an independent idea (3.2.1). Fifth, the conception of a sign that Saussure employs is not only not a plausible candidate for one of signs in general, but assumes uncritically that signs are double entities. So even assuming that Saussure thought that his key distinctions could be derived from his primordial principles together with his conception of a sign, it is difficult to see that the derivation as such could be of much interest.

No doubt Saussure's actual argument is much less tidy if, as I have suggested, most of the time he followed the second modest strategy. But his contribution of the reorientation of the study of language was, for all that, epoch-making. It marked a decisive reorientation in the history of linguistics. And if distinctions such as that between *langue* and *parole* cannot be derived from the first principles of an ambitious over-arching theory, they are none the worse for that. The real test of their worth is the use that they can be put to in the articulation of a theory of language that makes the development of a coherent, criticisable methodology for its study possible; and Saussure's distinctions certainly did that.

NOTES

1. Saussure's work: its context and significance

1. The first page reference is to the second edition of *Cours de linguistique générale*, the pagination of which is retained in other editions, including de Mauro's critical edition (*TM*); the second reference is to Wade Baskin's translation. Though the page numbering of Harris's translation is different from either, the corresponding page of *CLG* is always indicated there, so that it is possible to identify the relevant page of his translation.
2. My discussion is particularly indebted to that of Chapter 1 of Ducrot 1968, which very clearly illustrates the value of placing Saussure in a historical context. See also Culler 1976, ch. 3. A sympathetic account of the biological analogies developed by nineteenth-century linguists can be found in Sampson 1980, ch. 1.
3. For a discussion of this see Chomsky 1966; Ducrot 1968, ch. 1; Ducrot and Todorov 1972; Culler 1976, ch. 3.
4. The argument, in brief, is that since a given state of a language is the unintentional by-product of individual speech acts, and since its signs depend on their place within it, the latter are arbitrary in the sense that they are historically constituted without being designed or planned (5.2).
5. Although, as I said, it is not easy to see how the mixture could have been avoided altogether, there is at least one major respect in which the editors' way of combining the two terminologies is unfortunate. In the first explanation given of a sign they retain Saussure's discarded explanation of a sign as the union of two things, an acoustic

image and a concept, even though the latter term has individualistic psychological connotations which are very misleading from the point of view of the theory that Saussure goes on to develop, and quite apart from the fact that the term has no intrinsic connections with the term 'system'. It is true that later the new terms 'signifier' and 'signified' are introduced by the editors to replace the pair originally used.

> Ambiguity would disappear if the three notions involved here were designated by three names, each suggesting and opposing the others. I propose to retain the word *sign* [*signe*], to designate the whole and to replace *concept* and *sound-image* respectively by *signified* [*signifié*] and *signifier* [*signifiant*]: the last two terms have the advantage of indicating the opposition that separated them from each other and from the whole of which they are parts. (*CLG*, 99, 67)

This passage suggests that, apart from the advantage of an implied relationship, the two new terms have close family relationships with the pair they replace, so that a signified is a concept. But in fact the new terminology has radically different theoretical implications from the old (6.1).

6. Examination of the sources reveals that this is yet another place at which the initiative of the editors has been considerable. Apart from the fact that the italicisation is their responsibility, for some reason they discard the metaphor of the study of *langue* as a platform from which one can view the position of other aspects of language (*langage*). The metaphor is found in the notes of all the students. For instance, Madame Sechehaye writes: '[It is] when one accords first place to *la langue*, making it the point of departure, that one can give their true place to the other elements of language (*langage*)' (Engler 1, 30B). This certainly makes the study of *la langue* central, in that it is the foundation of any kind of study of language, but there is no suggestion that it is its own raison d'être 'in and for itself'. So the italicised passage read in relation to its sources can hardly be used to underwrite the interpretive summary of the whole of *CLG* encapsulated in the final remarks.

7. As de Mauro points out, this order of presentation, which stresses the interdependence of the study of languages and of language itself, corresponded to a deep conviction of Saussure's which he articulated in his 1891 inaugural lecture at Geneva:

> ... the most elementary linguistic phenomena will not be surmised or clearly perceived, classified, and understood unless one resorts in the first and last instance to the study of languages.... On the other hand, to want to study languages ignoring the fact that they are governed primordially by certain principles which are summarised in the idea of language (*langage*) is a task even more bereft of any serious significance, of any genuine scientific foundation. (*TM*, 354)

8. Here is a detailed comparison of the relevant passages:

Third Course	CLG
(A)	
Pt II: *Language (la langue)*	Introduction:
Ch. I: *La langue* distinguished from *langage*	Ch. 3: The object of linguistics; ch. 4: Linguistics of language and linguistics of speaking
(B)	
Ch. II: Nature of the linguistic sign	Pt 1: General principles Ch. 1: Nature of the linguistic sign
Ch. II': Immutability and mutability of the sign	Ch. 2: The same
Ch. II'': Static and historical linguistics	Ch. 3: The same Pt 2: Synchronic linguistics Ch. 1: Generalities [= (H)(i)]
(E)	
Ch. III: The concrete entities of language	Ch. 2: The same Ch. 3: Identities, realities, values [in part based on (E)]
(F)	
Ch. 4: The abstract entities of language	Ch. 4: Linguistic value [in part based on (H)(iii)]
(G)	
Ch. V: Absolute and relative arbitrariness	Ch. 5: Associative and syntagmatic relations [in part based on (H)(ii)]
(H)	
Ch. VI: Static linguistics (i) Generalities (*SM* III, 140–1)	Ch. 6: Mechanisms of language [6.1 is in part based on (H) (ii); 6.3 on (G)]
(ii) Syntagmatic and associative relations (*SM* III, 142–7)	Ch. 7: Grammar and its subdivisions [based entirely on the Second Course]
(iii) Values of terms and senses of words (*SM* III, 148ff)	Ch. 8: Role of abstract entities in grammar [= F]

9. Not everyone would agree about the importance of these issues. Harris, for instance, writes, 'The question then is – and has been for many years – how to make sense of reading this Saussure who is the presumptive author of the *Cours*; not whether what we read is a correct or incorrect account of "what the real Saussure really meant". For whatever that may have been is arguably irrecoverable anyway' (1987, viii). He goes on to argue that even if the Saussure of *CLG* were a literary fabrication of the editors, he would be none the worse for that; after all, 'so might Socrates, conceivably, be a fabrication of Plato's' (ibid.).

2. The distinction between *langue* and *parole*

1. This is not an uncontroversial position. Culler, for instance, takes a different view; see 1976, 34.

2. Often to talk of a discipline's object is to talk about the entities whith which it is exclusively concerned, together with their essential properties. However, as de Mauro argues, the term 'object' does not always have a material interpretation, as in 'What objects are being talked about?' (*TM*, 414). Sometimes to talk about the object of a discipline is to talk about what it seeks to explain. On this view, to argue that *langue* is the object of linguistics is to argue that when linguistic explanations are given, pride of place must be given to the reconstruction of the *langue* (= underlying set of conventions) of a language; but it does not follow that linguistic explanations are concerned only with facts about *langue*. To explain how a particular *langue* is constituted, how it changes, and how it is acquired, recourse may be necessary to facts of a quite different kind – ones of *parole* (2.1.3). This is the interpretation of 'object' needed for a proper understanding of Saussure's thesis that *langue* is the object of linguistics.

3. There is a fourth term waiting to be fitted in also, viz. the individual language faculty – *faculté du langage*.

4. This is not because I believe that a good command of French will enable one to see easily what Saussure's distinctions really are; on the contrary, he often uses ordinary words in a technical way. The point is to ensure that it is always clear which of the three key terms he has in mind.

5. For a discussion see Lyons 1968, 99ff. The first description would be the subject matter of phonetics; the second, of phonology; so speech sounds are the subject matter of the first discipline, whereas it is the latter which is concerned with the functionally significant features of the sounds. For instance, Lyons points out that in English *p*, *t*, and *k* in certain positions are slightly aspirated; but that while this is of interest to phonetics, it is of no interest to phonology, since 'the distinction between the aspirated and the unaspirated variety never has the function of keeping apart different words in English (this is a very crude, and partly inaccurate, statement that will be treated more fully later); it is not a *functional* difference: it is a phonetic difference, but not a phonological, or phonemic difference of English' (p. 100).

   I follow the convention which represents a phonetic description of a speech sound by using square brackets, e.g. [nu]; a phonological description is represented thus: /nu/.

6. For discussion of these issues and of the inadequacies of articulatory and acoustic phonetics see Jakobson 1978, Lecture 1. Reporting the work of Menzerath and Lacerda, Jakobson comments on its implications for articulatory phonetics:

   > As for the speech chain, they arrived at an even more paradoxical conclusion. From a strictly articulatory point of view

there is no *succession* of sounds.... However interesting or important the study of linguistic sounds in their purely motor aspect may be everything indicates to us that such a study is no more than an auxiliary tool for linguistics, and that we must look elsewhere for the principles by which the phonic matter of language are organised. (p. 11)

He goes on to maintain that acoustic phonetics fares no better than articulatory phonetics in providing principles of individuation:

Acoustics can provide us, in impressive detail, with the micrographic image of each sound, but it cannot interpret this image; it is not in a position to make use of its own results. It is as if they were the hieroglyphics of an unknown language. When, as is always the case, two sounds show both similarities and dissimilarities, acoustics, having no intrinsic criteria for distinguishing what is significant from what is not, has no way of knowing whether it is the similarity or the dissimilarity which is crucial in any given case. It cannot tell whether it is a case of two variants of one sound or of two different sounds. (p. 19)

Jakobson goes on to argue that this shows that 'we must ask what is the immediate aim of sounds, considered as acoustic phenomena? In raising the question we straight away go beyond the level of the signifier, beyond the domain of sound as such, and we enter the domain of the signified, the domain of meaning' (ibid.).

7. For a different interpretation see Harris 1987, 39.
8. Whether Saussure should have used this argument is another matter. It seems to imply that speech and writing are, or at least could be, simply different ways of articulating the same language. But this conflicts with the view that writing is a parasitic system and not even part of the province of linguistics.
9. Some of the things that might have been included and that Saussure lists are: 'the pure acoustical sensation, the identification of that sensation with the latent sound-image, the muscular image of phonation, etc.' (*CLG*, 28, 12). Interestingly, there is no reference to whatever thoughts either person might be having. Suppose, for instance, A wanted to ask B for the time. Why should A opt for a particular way of formulating the request, e.g., 'Have you got the time?', rather than for one of the many other possible ways: 'Can you tell me the time?', 'What time is it?', 'I'd like to know the time', etc.? The model envisages the encoding of thoughts but gives no account of the way in which they are formulated.
10. The text is far from clear, and it is possible that he did not mean to count (i) as active and (v) as passive. In both cases all that is involved is an 'unlocking', so that distinguishing them as respectively active and passive seems arbitrary. On the other hand, he clearly does want to say that reception is passive, for this is central to his argument.
11. It is true that we have to wait for an account of this until later, in fact until Part 2, Chapter 5; but the role staked out for it is clear

in outline. It is that faculty which enables B not merely to associate with a given sound image the same concept as does A, but also to relate the linguistic units identified in the same structurally significant ways, so that for instance B understands 'The dog bit the boy' to say that it was the dog that bit the boy, and not vice versa. For detailed discussion see 5.3.

12. The concept of generation is used here in the technical sense of modern linguistics in which a grammar is said to generate a sentence, and does not, therefore, imply anything about the corresponding performance. In fact Saussure does not always count sentences as units of *parole*. This is an issue which reveals considerable tension in his thought; but I argue later that there is no doubt that he was committed to treating sentences as part of *langue* and that he had worked out a way of doing this in principle, though certainly not in detail (5.3.2). However, since this is controversial, for the time being I shall treat his claim that the sentence is not a unit of *langue* as his considered view.

13. What Saussure meant by 'phonology' was not concerned with the functionally significant features of sounds but with their articulation, i.e., with what falls now within the province of phonetics. That is why he treated phonology in his sense of the term as an auxiliary science. By 'phonetics' he meant the study of the evolution of speech sounds.

14. It should be said that despite apparently conceding that an orthographic representation can be as direct as an acoustic one, Lyons argues for the priority of phonic substance (1968, 65).

15. If there were such a system, then the theoretical slack between the written and the spoken forms would be completely taken up, and we would no longer have to worry about how accurate a guide the former was to the latter.

3. Language as a system of signs, I: Signs, arbitrariness, linearity, and change

1. As Harris points out, a nomenclaturist might maintain (i) that there are language-independent objects without maintaining that there are language-independent ideas; (ii) that signs are psychological; and (iii) that the relation between a name and what it names is indirect, in that it is mediated by a sense (1987, 57).

2. Indeed, it is arguable that he went further and maintained that there are no language-independent concepts, so turning the position of the *Port Royal Grammar* on its head (Ducrot 1968, 46). However, since the rejection of the comparativists' claim does not require such a strong claim as this, we shall ignore it here.

3. His psychologistic stance is *prima facie* highly questionab... ven if a sign's intralinguistic relations are meaning-determining and it is knowledge of them which enables members of the linguistic community to communicate with each other, it does not follow that the relations in question have to be psychological ones holding between

psychological entities. If the relations are meaning-determining, all that is necessary for members of the linguistic community to communicate is that they should have similar representations of them, not that the relations in question be ones relating psychological entities.

4. The extent to which the new terminology has radical theoretical implications which the original does not is clear from a discussion later in *CLG*. Writing of signs as the union of a signifier and a signified, Saussure says:

> We constantly risk grasping only a part of the entity and thinking we are embracing it in its totality; this would happen, for example, if we divided the spoken chains into syllables, for the syllable has no value except in phonology [= modern phonetics]. A succession of sounds is linguistic only if it supports an idea. Considered independently, it is material for a physiological study, and nothing more than that.
>
> The same is true of the signified aˢ soon as it is separated from its signifier. Considered independently, concepts like 'house', 'white', 'see', etc. belong to psychology. They become linguistic entities only when associated with sound-images; in language a concept is a quality of its phonic substance just as a particular slice of sound is a quality of the concept. (*CLG*, 144, 103)

5. But it is worth noting that it is one thing to maintain that there are no language-independent meanings, and another to maintain that signifiers belonging to different languages cannot have the same meaning. The second claim follows from the first only if it is impossible for the signifiers to have the same meaning-determining relations in their respective languages.

If I understand him, Benveniste has a different objection, namely that to make his point Saussure has to introduce a third term, 'reality', as well as the two in question, the signifier and its signified; but this is illegitimate if language is aˈ form and not a substance (1966, 50). Though Benveniste is right to say that Saussure's concept of motivation takes into account the relation between something non-linguistic, e.g., a cuckoo, and its signifier and signified, the concept is used to make a point central to his overall theory, namely that there is nothing extralinguistic which determines the nature of signifiers and signifieds. It is hard to see how such a point could be made without doing what Benveniste says is illegitimate, namely discuss the relations among signifiers, signifieds, and reality.

6. The point is well made in Burge 1975 that we must not so define the conventional that for a convention C to exist there must also exist an alternative C', which those who comply with C could adopt here and now, as things are. What is required instead, as Burge points out, is that it be true that there is an alternative C' which, if established, would have served the same purposes and which the persons in question could have learned to conform to at an appropriate stage of their development. For instance, once I have

learned to speak English with a Yorkshire accent I may find it impossible to speak it with any other. But that does not mean that my accent does not rest on usage and convention. Presumably a different usage would have served broadly the same purposes, and had I been exposed to it when a child I would have had a different accent.

7. Someone who would quarrel with this conclusion is Jakobson. See 1978, 113.

8. Similarly, one could, as presumably Chomsky would, agree about the marginality of onomatopoeia and interjections, and argue that there is something external to a particular language, namely the faculty of language, which motivates various features of it.

9. It might be argued that the numerical example is poorly chosen, since the structure of the number descriptions in the language is determined by the structure of the system of cardinal numbers. It seems to me that this underestimates the idiosyncrasies of natural language number systems. For instance, *dix-sept* is structure-revealing, but *seize* is not, and *quatre-vingts* has a structure which is not linguistically productive. Anyway, there are non-numerical examples, e.g., *poirier, cerisier, pommier*, etc. (*CLG*, 181, 131).

10. A good review and evaluation of these discussions is to be found in Harris 1987, 69ff.

11. The relevant passage is *CLG*, 146, 104; it is discussed in 5.1.

12. I owe this point to John Rae.

4. Language as a system of signs, II: Diachronic and synchronic linguistics

1. It is worth observing that at least one of the metaphors that Saussure uses to illuminate the notion of a value, the economic metaphor, does not sit very comfortably with the idea of linguistic values as pure values (6.2).

2. Saussure says that 'changes are always unintentional, whilst the synchronic fact is always significant' (*CLG*, 122, 85). This runs together two different contrasts. On the one hand, he wants to say that synchronic facts are always concerned with values, whereas diachronic ones are not. But he also wants to deny that diachronic changes are intended to produce the overall systematic effects they have. However, the rather curious remark about life being breathed into differences suggests that he may have thought that values ultimately do depend on intentions, e.g., on the collective will to find some means of expressing the plural.

3. The other two analogies are the projection of an object onto a plane surface and the difference between the structure revealed when a plant is cut first transversely and then longitudinally (*CLG*, 125, 87).

4. In the case of chess, a state of the game may be defined as an arrangement of pieces produced by a legitimate series of moves from a given initial state. Clearly, no analogous explanation of what constitutes a state of a given language is available.

5. Lepschy makes a similar point: '...there is a sense in which some "diachronic" information is included in the rules of chess: one might need to know whether the king or rook has moved, if one wants to castle; one may need to know whether a pawn has just been moved if one wants to take it *en passant*; and to decide whether a game ends in a draw one needs to know whether the same position occurs for the third time; or in the end game one may need to know how many moves have been made from a certain moment onwards' (1970, 46).

6. Moreover, this response ignores the fact that in many states competent players would make the same move, since what is a good move is determined by the nature and purpose of the game and the state in question. So in a given state of a game of chess played to win, certain moves are much more likely than others. But then why in a particular language state should there not be developments which are more likely than others? For instance, in the example discussed in 4.2, the fortuitous existence of two different ways of marking the plural at Stage 2 in the case of the nouns in question might make it more likely that sooner or later one or the other of these would be used to mark the plural rather than some completely different form. Lepschy makes a similar point: 'As traditional linguistics used to repeat, language is in fact continuously changing, even though the speaker may not be conscious of it and may translate such changes as he experiences in terms of stylistic choices between synchronically coexistent uses' (1970, 45).

7. That signs are concrete rather than abstract objects is a fundamental part of Saussure's theory. This is so because they 'are realities that have their seat in the brain' (*CLG*, 32, 15). Moreover, they are tangible in the rather peculiar sense that they can be 'reduced to conventional written symbols', so that if a language is a storehouse of sound images, writing is its tangible form (ibid.). For further discussion see 5.1.

8. Full discussion of this issue would take us too far afield. But, as Harris points out in an insightful discussion of Saussure's theoretical difficulties, he cannot allow individuals too much freedom over analogical creation, because that would leave little or no explanatory role for *langue*. On the other hand, he cannot overcircumscribe their freedom, because in that case their only role would be to implement changes implicit in a given state: 'Why are these extremes uncongenial from a Saussurean point of view? Because in the one case *langue* merges with *parole*, and in the other synchrony merges with diachrony' (Harris 1987, 152).

5. Language as a system of signs, III: Identities, system, and relations

1. The principle would presumably rule that one cannot treat 'is ——ing', which has the present continuous tense as its signified, as an element of 'is running'. For an interesting discussion see Harris 1987, 111.

2. It is possible that Saussure's position about the psychological reality of abstract entities was not fully worked out. For instance, in the Third Course he expresses puzzlement about the point of the distinction between concrete and abstract entities. To consider an idea apart from its signifier is to consider it as an abstraction; but, he goes on to say, 'nothing in *langue* can be abstract if one takes the concrete to be everything present to the consciousness of the speaking subject' (*SM*, 84).

   The possibility that a grammarian's analysis might involve distinctions not made by the native speaker is discussed in the appendix to Parts 3 and 4 of *CLG*. This discussion contrasts two sorts of analysis, the first called objective, which is made by grammarians, and the second called subjective, which involves only distinctions recognisable by the speaker. Saussure acknowledges that the two sorts of analysis might diverge, but argues that they are equally legitimate. This is certainly a puzzling remark, since it seems to imply that an objective study is not necessarily one of *langue*. However, it may be that the views in question were ones he abandoned; the material for the appendix comes from the First Course.

3. For an extended discussion of this and other sorts of difficulty see Ducrot 1968, 48, and Harris 1987, 108ff.

4. The material discussed here is largely drawn from Part 2, Chapter 3, of *CLG*.

5. The material drawn on in this section comes almost entirely from Chapters 5 and 6 of Part 2 of *CLG*. In these chapters the initiatives of the editors were considerable. For instance, the expression 'the set of phonic and conceptual differences' occurring in the first sentence of Chapter 6 has no warrant in the text (Engler 2, 290). The main effect of the editorial initiatives is the compression of material which is much clearer in the notes than it is in their text.

6. The term 'discourse' is the editors'; in their notes the students all use *parole*.

7. The examples are mine, but they are based on the ones Saussure uses; cf. Engler 2, 280.

8. This was not a slip, for later we read: 'This notion of a syntagm can be applied to unities of whatever kind; as much as to simple words as complex ones and sentences' (Engler 2, 283).

9. Arguing that these relations are interdependent, Lyons writes that the 'defining characteristic of modern "structural" linguistics is as follows: linguistic units have no validity independently of their paradigmatic and syntagmatic relations with other units' (1968, 75). Lyons uses the term 'paradigmatic' instead of Saussure's 'associative'. It should be said, though, that Lyons denies that syntagmatic relations are necessarily sequential or time-ordered.

   If there is an answer to the argument of 3.3 that it cannot be true that the whole mechanism of language depends on the principle of Linearity – even on Saussure's own account, since associative relations are not linear – then it would, as far as I can see, have to appeal to the interdependence of the two types of relation. But even so the principle would seem to be false if Lyons is right that syntagmatic relations are not necessarily sequential.

10. This consists of a remark to the effect that we should recognise in *contre/marche* a relation between its parts (*contre* and *marche*), and also a part–whole relation, viz. that between *contre*, *marche*, and *contremarche*. In the first case we are concerned with a relation of succession; and in the second, one which is productive in the sense that *contremarche* has to be seen as the product of its parts (Engler 2, 283).

6. Language as a system of signs, IV: Values, differences, and reality

1. The order in which I discuss these is that of the Third Course, which is the reverse of *CLG*.
2. If Saussure is right, *mouton* doubles as a count noun and a bulk term. For some reason, 'sheep' does not, though 'lamb' does – compare 'Mary had a little lamb' with the continuations 'to eat' and 'which followed her to school one day'. Qua count noun, should we say that 'lamb' has the same signified as does 'lamb' qua bulk term? There are good Saussurean reasons for answering in the negative; the count noun is potentially modifiable in ways in which the bulk term is not, and vice-versa. Moreover, there are equally cogent reasons for distinguishing the signifieds of *mouton* in its two uses. So it is not clear why 'sheep' and *mouton* should not have the same signified provided the latter is not being used as a bulk term.
3. The diagram is a modification of one that appears in the students' notes:

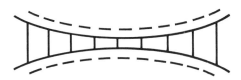

In this diagram *langue* is intermediate between thought and sound but is not a modification of either. The divisions introduced by *langue* are clearly not phonic on this model; it is not clear that they are not in the one devised by the editors.
4. The passage is in fact a much-compressed version of a longer one from the Second Course which the editors inserted into the Third Course at this point. One can see why they felt the need to insert some account of the origin of systems of values at this stage.
5. For a general discussion of these issues and of the theory of semantic fields see Lehrer 1974 and Lyons 1977, ch. 8.
6. For instance, I argued earlier that one of the defects of the way in which Saussure attempts to define the *langue/parole* distinction is that he assumes that there is a given field *langage* whose boundaries

are clear, so that it can be divided. On this account, *parole* is what is left when *langue* has been subtracted. But since we do not know precisely what belongs to *langage*, we do not know what the remainder is (2.1.3).

7. For a critical discussion of the view that underlying all vocabularies there is an unstructured thought mass or meaning substance see Lyons 1977, 259.

8. For a discussion and evaluation of it see Lyons 1977, 246.

9. Here 'phoneme' is being used in the modern sense for a sound which is linguistically functional. For a discussion see *TM*, nn. 236, 111. See also Lyons 1968, 99ff.

10. The clause begining 'it is even' is an addition of the editors'. The passage reveals considerable tension in Saussure's thought. The sign is said to be the union of a signifier and signified, and is as such a concrete entity. From this point of view, to consider the signifier or signified in isolation is to consider it as an abstraction. On the other hand, Saussure argues that a *langue* is an association of two independent orders of differences which, as Caws says, 'stresses the incommensurability, perhaps the mutual inaccessibility of the two domains, which have no essential connection but only an arbitrary and artificially forced association' (1988, 75).

11. It is important to note that the idea of a lexical field, which is important for linguistics, does not presuppose that anything is given. Consider, for instance, Lyons's explanation of a lexical field:

> Lexemes and other units that are semantically related, whether paradigmatically [= Saussure's 'associatively'] or syntagmatically, within a given language system can be said to belong to, or to be members of, the same (semantic) field; and a field whose members are lexemes is a lexical field. A lexical field is therefore a paradigmatically and syntagmati-cally structured subset of the vocabulary (or lexicon). (1977, 268)

Clearly, this account does not assume that the field is given. On the contrary, what fields there are depends on what paradigmatic and syntagmatic relations there are between lexemes.

12. This is not, however, always true; there is surely a systematic difference between 'butcher' and 'baker' within the domain of occupations, and between 'bite' and 'scratch' in the domain of aggressive acts, yet 'X is a butcher' does not imply 'X is not a baker' any more than 'X bit Mary' implies 'X did not scratch Mary'. Great care is needed in stating a rule that covers cases like these or, indeed, applies to other tenses and verbs; for instance, 'X will be hot' does not imply 'X will not be cold' any more than 'X went on Saturday' implies 'X did not go on Tuesday' (Lehrer 1974, 25).

13. These are not meant to be exhaustive. For a more detailed discussion see Lyons 1977, ch. 9, and Lehrer 1974, ch. 2. Of particular interest is the type of opposition which Lyons calls 'directional'. This

is seen most clearly in the relationship which holds between 'up': 'down', 'arrive': 'depart', and 'come': 'go'. What these pairs have in common, in what might be regarded as their most typical usage, is an implication of motion in one of two opposed directions with respect to a given place P. (1977, 281)

The challenge from the point of view of structuralist semantics would be to account for the apparently essential way in which the use of these terms involves reference to a position.

14. For a discussion of the terms 'marked' and 'unmarked' see Lyons 1977, 305. The binarist would of course have to explain how to reduce the many apparently non-binary contrasts there are to sets of binary contrasts.

7. Successes and failures

1. Of course the tradition which has influenced Quine's views is not structuralism but pragmatism, and in particular the work of Dewey. Even so, Dewey reached a number of conclusions which would have been congenial to Saussure. For Dewey, 'language is specifically a mode of interaction of at least two beings, a speaker and a hearer; it presupposes an organized group from which they have acquired their habits of speech. It is, therefore, a relationship' (1958, 185). On the other hand, Dewey and Quine's behaviourism would not have been acceptable to Saussure.

2. For a detailed discussion of this see Gibson 1982 and Gochet 1986.

3. Roughly speaking, the difference between underdetermination and indeterminacy is that whilst in the first case the data are compatible with different hypotheses, nevertheless one of them is correct; in the second this is not so. In other words, in the first case there is a fact of the matter; in the second there is none.

4. For Quine's conception of an observation sentence see Gochet 1986, 32-4, 44-6.

5. For valuable discussions of the issues involved see O'Neill 1973 and MacDonald & Pettit 1981.

6. The latter suggestion has some historical provenance. Louis Caille, for instance, claimed that the comparison Saussure makes of linguistic value with forms of exchange was suggested by Tarde's *Psychologie économique*; others have suggested that the distinction between *langue* and *parole* is to be found in Tarde's *Lois de l'imitation*.

7. For a valuable and very fair discussion of this issue see D'Agostino 1986, 37ff.

8. A fuller, though still somewhat abbreviated, version of his analysis is as follows:

A regularity R is a convention in a population P, if and only if, within P

(1) Everyone conforms to R.

(2) Everyone believes that the others conform to R.

(3) The belief that the others conform to R gives everyone a good and decisive reason to conform to R himself.

(4) There is a general preference for general conformity to R rather than slighly-less-than-general-conformity – in particular conformity by all but any one.

(5) There is at least one alternative regularity R' which is such that the beliefs that the others conformed to R' would give everyone a decisive reason to conform to R'.

(6) (1)–(5) are matters of mutual knowledge: they are known to everyone, it is known to everyone that they are known to everyone, and so on. (Lewis 1975, 5)

9. The role of the mutual-knowledge conditions in Lewis's account is not uncontroversial. Burge has argued convincingly that the exis-tence of an alternative need not be mutually known:

> Imagine a small, isolated, unenterprising linguistic community none of whose members ever heard anyone's speaking differently. Such a community would not know – or perhaps have reason to believe – that there are humanly possible alternatives to speaking their language.... Yet we have no inclination to deny that their language is conventional. (Burge 1975, 250)

Furthermore, in Lewis's detailed analysis (n. 8 above), provided conditions (2) and (3) are satisfied, everyone has a reason to conform whether or not (6) is satisfied. But perhaps without (6) that reason would be a weak one.

10. For a discussion of semiology and linguistics see Barthes 1967; Chomsky 1969, ch. 3; Robey 1973; Culler 1976, ch. 4; Leiber 1978; Caws 1988.

11. Quite how this is to be done in detail is not clear, but Culler has suggested the broad lines which such a derivation might take:

> Saussure's notes suggest [that] the distinction between *langue* and *parole* is a logical and necessary consequence of the arbitrary nature of the sign and the problem of identity in linguistics. In brief: if the sign is arbitrary, then, as we have seen, it is a purely relational entity, and if we wish to define and identify signs we must look to the system of relations and distinctions which create them. We must therefore distinguish between the various substances in which signs are manifested and the actual forms which constitute signs; and when we have done this what we have isolated is a system of forms which underlies actual linguistic behavior or manifestation. The system of forms is *la langue;* the attempt to study signs leads us, inexorably, to take this as the proper object of linguistic investigation. (1976, 34)

However, for reasons given later in this chapter, this derivation would seem to be somewhat shaky.

12. These examples are only suggestions. But an examination of the design features of language does not encourage either the idea that it is just one sign system amongst many or the idea that study of other sign systems will throw a great deal of light on it (Lyons 1977).

BIBLIOGRAPHY

Sources and texts

Saussure, Ferdinand de. 1916. *Cours de linguistique générale*, edited by Charles Bally and Albert Sechehaye, with the collaboration of Albert Riedlinger. Lausanne and Paris. (Page references are to the second edition of 1922, cited as *CLG*. This pagination is retained by subsequent editions, including de Mauro's critical edition.)

1972. *Cours de linguistique générale*. Critical edition, edited by Tullio de Mauro. Paris: Payot. (Cited as *TM*)

1977. *Course in General Linguistics*, translated by Wade Baskin. Glasgow: Fontana/Collins. (Cited as *WB*)

1986. *Course in General Linguistics*, translated by Roy Harris. La Salle, Ill.: Open Court.

Engler, Rudolf. 1967. *Cours de linguistique genérále: édition critique.* 3 fascicules, continuously paginated. Wiesbaden: Otto Harrassowitz. (Cited as *Engler*. The left-hand column gives the text of *CLG*, and the other five its sources, which are referred to by use of 'B' to 'F'. Thus 'Engler 2, 148 F' refers to the last column of p. 148 in the second fascicule.)

Godel, Robert. 1954. 'Notes inédites de F. de Saussure'. *Cahiers F. de Saussure* 12, 49–71.

1957. *Les sources manuscrites du cours de linguistique générale*. Geneva: Librairie Droz. (Cited as *SM*)

Godel, Robert (ed.). 1969. *A Geneva School Reader in Linguistics*. Bloomington: Indiana University Press.

Other works cited

Aarsleff, H. 1967. *The Study of Language in England, 1760–1860*. Princeton, N.J.: Princeton University Press.

Amacker, R. 1975. *Linguistique saussurienne*. Geneva and Paris: Librairie Droz.

Barthes, R. 1967. *Elements of Semiology*, translated by A. Lavers and C. Smith. New York: Hill and Wang.

Benveniste, E. 1966. *Problèmes de linguistique générale*. Paris: Gallimard.

Berlin, B., and P. Kay. 1970. *Basic Color Terms*. Berkeley and Los Angeles: University of California Press.

Burge, T. 1975. 'On Knowledge and Convention'. *Philosophical Review* 84, 249–55.

Calvet, L. 1975. *Pour et contre Saussure*. Paris: Payot.

Caws, P. 1988. *Structuralism: The Art of the Intelligible*. Atlantic Highlands, N.J.: Humanities Press.

Chomsky, N. 1957. *Syntactic Structures*. The Hague: Mouton.

1964. *Current Issues in Linguistic Theory*. The Hague: Mouton.

1965. *Aspects of the Theory of Syntax*. Cambridge, Mass.: MIT Press.

1966. *Cartesian Linguistics: A Chapter in the History of Rationalist Thought*. New York: Harper and Row.

1969. *Language and Responsibility*. Hassocks: Harvester.

Culler, J. 1976. *Saussure*. Glasgow: Fontana/Collins.

D'Agostino, F. 1986. *Chomsky's System of Ideas*. Oxford: Clarendon Press.

Danto, A. C. 1973. 'Methodological Individualism and Methodological Socialism'. In O'Neill 1973, 312–37.

Derrida, J. 1976. *Of Grammatology*, translated by G. C. Spivak. Baltimore: Johns Hopkins University Press.

1981. *Positions*, translated and annotated by A. Bass. London: Athlone.

Dewey, J. 1958. *Experience and Nature*. La Salle, Ill.: Open Court.

Doroszewski, W. 1933. 'Quelques remarques sur les rapports de la sociologie et de la linguistique', *Journal de Psychologie*.

Ducrot, O. 1968. *Le structuralisme en linguistique*. Paris: Seuil.

Ducrot, O., and T. Todorov. 1972. *Dictionnaire encyclopédique des sciences du langage*. Paris: Seuil.

Durkheim, E. 1982. *The Rules of Sociological Method*, edited with an introduction by S. Lukes; translated by W. D. Halls. London: Macmillan.

1952. *Suicide: A Study in Sociology*, translated by J. A. Spaulding and G. Simpson. London: Macmillan.

Firth, J. R. 1957. *Papers in Linguistics*. Oxford: Oxford University Press.

Gibson, R. F. 1982. *The Philosophy of W. V. Quine*. Tampa: University of South Florida.

Giddens, A. 1978. *Durkheim*. Hassocks: Harvester.

Gochet, P. 1986. *Ascent to Truth: A Critical Examination of Quine's Philosophy*. Munich: Philosophia Verlag.

Goffman, E. 1972. *Relations in Public*. Harmondsworth: Penguin.

Harris, R. 1987. *Reading Saussure*. London: Duckworth.

Henry, A. 1970. 'La linéarité du signifiant'. In J. Dierickx and Y. Lebrun (eds.), *Linguistique contemporaine: hommage à Eric Buyssens*. Brussels: Editions de L'Institut de Sociologie, 86–92.

Jakobson, R. 1978. *Six Lectures on Sound and Meaning*, translated by J. Mepham. Hassocks: Harvester.

Lehrer, A. 1974. *Semantic Fields and Lexical Structure*. Amsterdam: North-Holland.

Leiber, J. 1978. *Structuralism: Skepticism and Mind in the Psychological Sciences*. Boston: Twayne.

Lepschy, G. C. 1970. *A Survey of Structural Linguistics*. London: Faber and Faber.

Lévi-Strauss, C. 1977. *Structural Anthropology*, translated by C. Jacobson and B. Grundfest Schoepf. Harmondsworth: Penguin.

Lewis, D. 1975. 'Language and Languages'. In K. Gunderson (ed.), *Language, Mind and Knowledge*. Minnesota Studies in the Philosophy of Science, VII. Minneapolis: University of Minnesota Press, 3–35.

Lukes, S. 1973. *Durkheim*. London: Allen Lane.

Lyons, J. 1968. *An Introduction to Theoretical Linguistics*. Cambridge: Cambridge University Press.

1977. *Semantics*, vol. 1. Cambridge: Cambridge University Press.

MacDonald, G., and P. Pettit. 1981. *Semantics and Social Science*. London: Routledge and Kegan Paul.

Mill, J. S. 1875. *A System of Logic*, 9th ed. London: Longman.

Mounin, G. 1968. *Saussure ou le structuralisme sans le savoir*. Paris: Editions Seghers.

O'Neill, J. (ed.). 1973. *Modes of Individualism and Collectivism*. London: Heinemann.

Robey, D. (ed.). 1973. *Structuralism: An Introduction*. Oxford: Clarendon Press.

Quine, W. V. 1960. *Word and Object*. New York: Wiley.

1969. *Ontological Relativity and Other Essays*. New York: Columbia University Press.

1977. 'Facts of the Matter'. In R. S. Shahan and C. Swoyer (eds.), *Essays in the Philosophy of Quine*. Hassocks: Harvester, 155–69.

Sampson, G. 1980. *Schools of Linguistics: Competition and Evolution*. London: Hutchinson.

Schleicher, F. 1869. *Darwinism Tested by the Science of Language*, translated by A. Bikkers. London: Hotten.

Trier, J. 1931. *Der deutsche Wortschatz im Sinnbezirk des Verstandes*. Heidelberg: Winter.

1934. 'Das sprachliche Feld', *Jahrbuch für Deutsche Wissenschaft* 10.

Watkins, J. 1973. 'Ideal Types and Historical Explanation'. In O'Neill 1973, 143–65.

Index

Harris, R., 41–2, 48, 58–9, 163, 166, 169
historical linguistics, *see* comparative linguistics
Hjelmslev, L., 44, 137

identity, synchronic, 22, 92, 95–7, 104–5, 119
interjections, 54

Jakobson, R., 52, 58, 60, 121–3, 132, 164–5

Kay, P., 117, 132

language, 4, 22–3, 134–5; autonomy of, 10–13, 17, 55, 65; comparison with chess, 76–8, 114–15, 139, 168–9; comparison with Morse Code, 34, 37, 44–5; comparison with a symphony, 33, 37, 44–5; faculty of, 23–4, 42–4, 168; and social facts, 8, 22, 27–30, 61–3, 65, 145–55; and thought, 112–15; *see also* abstract *and* concrete entities of language
langue, 15, 21–4, 26–30, 34–6, 44–5, 65–6, 84–7, 151–2; and associative and syntagmatic relations, 100–4; as a form, 36–9, 112–15; and *parole*, 20–1, 33–4, 45–6, 137–9
Lehrer, A., 116, 128
Lepschy, G., 169
Lévi-Strauss, C., 5, 53, 102, 158
Lewis, D., 153–4, 173–4
lexical fields, 116–17, 172
linearity of the signifier, 56–61, 89, 94, 98, 137, 159
linguistics, 15, 17, 73, 134–7, 160; history of, 6–9; object of, 19–20, 22–3, 34–6, 46, 81, 84–5, 164; *see also* comparative, diachronic, structural, *and* synchronic linguistics
Lukes, S., 146
Lyons, J., 38, 94, 125–7, 130, 133, 164, 170, 172

Mauro, T. de, 14–15, 162, 164
Meillet, A., 144
methodological individualism, 147–9; and Saussurean linguistics, 149–52, 154–5

Mill, J. S., 147–8
Mounin, G., 5, 8, 144

Neo-Grammarians, 9
nomenclaturism, 11–12, 48–50, 66, 113, 142

onomatopoeia, 54
oppositions, linguistic, 110, 112, 121, 125–7; binary, 127–9

parole, 30–4, 84–5, 87, 138; and *langue*, 20–1, 45–6, 137–9
philosophers, Saussure's advice to, 9–13
phonemes, 120–3
Popper, K., 151
Port Royal Grammar, 10–12, 17, 55, 142, 166

Quine, W. V., 140–3

Rae, J., 168
Riedlinger, A., 13

Schleicher, F., 7–9
Sechehaye, A., 1, 13–16, 51, 136–7, 161–2, 170
semiology, 5–6, 17, 19, 35–6, 59, 61, 79, 83, 94, 98, 137, 155–60
signified, 14, 50–5, 108–11, 119, 162; and differences, 121–30
signifier, 14, 50–5, 56–61, 165; *see also* linearity of the signifier
signs, linguistic, 49–52, 155–60, *and see* arbitrary nature of the sign; form a system, 93–7, 108–10, 119, 125, 135; immutability of, 62–3; mutability of, 63–6; *see also* value: linguistic
social facts, 8, 27–8, 61–3, 135, 145–7; and Saussurean linguistics, 152–5
social realism, 143, 148; and Saussure, 152–5
speech sounds, 21–2, 40–3, 89, 164–5
structural linguistics, 104, 130, 170
structuralism, 5, 130, 135
synchronic linguistics, 17, 69–71, 74–8, 81–5, 134–5, 139; is really idiosynchronic, 82; *see also* identity, synchronic